Chipper is a beautiful story about overcoming adversity and such messages are important in all of our lives.

Richard Paul Evans
New York Times best selling author of The Christmas Box

Chipper is a story of home-town heroes. It illustrates the healing power of good families and friends and of caring professionals. It reminds us of the priceless value of life—every life. *Chipper* is a powerful story of fear, courage, frustration, friendship and hope. Thanks, neighbor, for sharing your inspiring story.

Michael O. Leavitt
Governor of Utah

"I never cease to marvel at the amazing power of children to recuperate from serious injury. I believe this has a lot to do with the power of positive thinking. Children want to be well and are not incumbered with the depression that often follows serious injuries in adults. Chip Mangum has an incredible desire to succeed. It is no wonder that he has recovered far better than any of us could have predicted. Along the way he has been a teacher, showing us the power and strength of the inner-self."

Marion L. Walker, M.D., F.A.C.S., F.A.A.P.
Professor and Head
Division of Pediatric Neurosurgery
University of Utah/Primary Children's Medical Center

"No teacher wants to fail, and when Chipper Mangum was seated before me in the classroom, I was determined to teach him. If I could bring light to a single idea within his mind and help him know success in learning in any way, I knew I too would have succeeded. What I did not know was that I would learn far more from this student than I could ever hope to teach him."

Gary Cowart
Cedar High School Math Instructor

What readers are saying about *Chipper*

Chipper held the attention of my class better than any book I have read to them—especially the boys! It opened the context to talk about some very important issues. Our class then raised two hundred sixty dollars for Primary Children's Medical Center.
  4th grade teacher [teacher of the year]

I started reading *Chipper* to my family for home evening and our kids voted to have home evening every night until we finished the book. We laughed, we cried, we talked. They wouldn't let me miss a night.
  Mother

Chipper really helped me understand how to help my dad after his brain injury. It gave me hope, courage and understanding.
  Adult daughter of a TBI victim.

Each night, I set a timer and my son must read for 20 minutes. *Chipper* is the first book he has ever read past the bell.
  Mother and teacher

We started the year by reading *Chipper*. Kids who hated writing are now keeping journals and writing great stuff!
  High school English teacher

For the first time since my stroke, I have thought about what my wife went through. Reading *Chipper* has made a big difference in our relationship. I'm recommending it to everyone.
  Stoke victim and president of a stroke victims support group

My class was riveted!
  Third grade teacher

I was reading *Chipper* out loud in the car and my dad made me stop. He couldn't see through his tears.
  16 year old girl

After reading *Chipper*, my twelve-year-old son said, "Mom, if you could find more books like this, I'd like reading!"
  Mother

Chipper

More than a Miracle

For Connie with love

From the diary of Sharron Mangum

Written by

Gayla Schmutz
alias Sharron Re
and
Lorraine Thompson

Drawings by Tom Baker

Chipper
More than a Miracle

While the following account is based on the diary of Sharron Mangum, some names have been changed and the incidents have been reconstructed fictionally.

Artwork: Tom Baker
Cover Design: Jeremy Wright
Printed in the United States of America
First Printing: June, 1997
Second Printing: December, 1997

Library of Congress Catalog Card Number 97-68941

ISBN: 1-56236-975-X

Distributed by Origin Book Sales, Inc.
Salt Lake City, Utah
800-748-4900

For Chipper

and all T.B.I. heroes and healers

Chapters

Authors' Note

Chipper Mangum is a pioneer. As the medical world expands it's capabilities, saving lives that would have been lost years—even months before, real people blaze the trails back to their home towns to face the challenge of living with the effects of their traumatic brain injuries [T.B.I.]. Real children return to their families and friends, to their classrooms and playgrounds. Chipper Mangum is one of these people. In the wake of his brain injuries, Chipper, his family, friends and community would all face uncharted territory. They are not alone. Brain trauma has been labeled "America's silent epidemic" claiming over 56,000 lives and disabling nearly 100,000 more Americans every year.* It is our hope that as you become acquainted with Chipper, the uncharted territory known as T.B.I. will not seem so foreboding.

There were far too many people involved in this project and in the story itself to recognize all adequately. We are confident they know how much we value each vital part.

We acknowledge the editing talent of our friend Steve Walker, who is an expert at turning muddle into meat. We also wish to recognize the efforts of Tom Baker who drew these sketches from actual pictures, adding an even greater depth of truth to the telling of Chipper's story.

We express special thanks to the Mangum family. For the past seven years, Sharron Mangum has recorded their day to day experiences. Exposing your personal life to others is not easy. It was her desire to educate and encourage that sparked this book. Thanks, Sharron, for giving us the opportunity to learn from you and your son.

We especially thank our friend, Chipper, who has strengthened and taught us in ways he may never realize. He is the hero of this story.

Love, Gayla and Lorraine   *http://www.biausa.org

Chipper

More than a Miracle

1

The Tree

"Relax, Mom. It's not like I've never done this before. We'll be back before dark with enough firewood to fill a barn."

Jason slapped a hand on his mom's shoulder and jumped behind the wheel of his dad's old '55 Chevy. A short blast on the horn brought Arron and his friend

Chipper

Chipper sprinting through the Ashworths' open door, lunches in hand. They hurdled the tailgate and waved to Jason and Cade through the window of the cab, signaling they were ready to pull out. Jason turned the key and the engine came to life. He flashed a satisfied smile across the seat to Cade.

"I've been planning this day since last fall when Dad and I first saw 'er. I don't know how long the old tree has been on that mountain, but today she's coming down!"

Jason's hand met Cade's for a high five, and they were off.

Chipper loved the mountains. Throwing his head back, he watched the towering aspens and ponderosas file by as the truck bobbled and jigged over the dirt road. He filled his lungs to bursting with spring air so fresh it tasted like pine. With a quick flip of his hand, he shoved the bill of his Little League cap to the rear, catcher style. A sudden dip threw the two boys in the back into a squirming heap. Laughing, they attempted to untangle themselves before the next jolt as the truck bounced up the hillside.

"I think he's taking a deer trail," Arron grimaced, rubbing his elbow.

Jason stuck his head out the window. "Someone hang on to that power saw," he hollered. "Dad'll kill me if that gets broken."

Arron grabbed hold of the saw and hollered back, "How much farther is it?"

"Just over that ridge."

"I don't think Jason even knows where he's going," Chipper grinned at Arron. "I'll bet he's lost and don't wanna admit it!"

The twelve-year-olds laughed out loud. Nothing beat poking fun at your best friend's big brother when he couldn't hear you.

"Watch for that huge tree," Chipper called. "From the sound of it, we should be able to see it from anywhere on Cedar Mountain."

The truck slowed down to straddle protruding lava rock, then sped over a sandy stretch. Slowing, speeding up, slowing again, they pulled up an incline and over to a level grassy spot.

"Everyone out!" Cade ordered. "All right, Ashworth, where's this monster of a tree?"

"Thar she stands, mate!" Jason turned proudly toward a gnarled and twisted ponderosa pine that pushed majestically between the quakies and spruce. The boys followed his pointed finger, eyeing the tree in awe where it loomed, half dead, dominating the hillside.

"Wow! Looks like some ancient ghost tree!" Arron declared. "It's so . . . old!"

"Did you think we'd cut down some baby pine for firewood? It's perfect!" Jason reached in the back for the saw and hoisted it over the endgate. "Just look up at all those dead branches and start counting dollar signs, boys."

"Let's eat first," Cade suggested. "Can't expect a man to work on an empty stomach."

"You guys go ahead if you want. I'll fell this baby and have some wood for you to stack before you're through."

"Yeah sure, Ashworth. That tree will take all morning to cut," Cade said, stuffing a doughnut in his mouth.

"Which way d'ya figure it'll fall?" Chipper wanted to know.

Jason eyed the giant ponderosa with an air of importance. "I'm going to cut that south side, where it leans a little. Then she'll fall that way." He nodded down the slope and leaned to give the cord of the chain-saw a jerk. Balancing the saw on his thigh, he grinned his approval when the motor sputtered to a rolling roar.

"What if it falls on the truck?" Arron asked.

"Like a tree's gonna fall uphill. It won't. That's why we parked where we did. No way I'd take any chances. Just be sure you guys stick by the truck when she's ready to fall, so you don't take any branches in the face—they'll be flying everywhere." Jason headed for the tree.

"Hey Chip," Arron called above the noise, licking a Twinkie wrapper. "Let's find something to knock the branches off that thing after it falls."

Chipper tossed his orange peels at Cade and headed after Arron to scout the area for limbs.

The moist earth squeezed under their feet as the two boys romped through the forest, each heading off in his own direction. Last fall's aspen leaves dotted the hillside like ancient gold coins. Chipper plopped down in a pile and gathered an armful of musty gold, tossing it into the air above him.

"Mine! All mine!" he yelled into the mountain air. He unsheathed a deadwood limb to duel with the outstretched arms of a quaking aspen.

The Tree

Deeper in the woods, he made his way through shadows split and splattered by the midmorning sunlight. Dew still hung on spiderwebs hidden in thickets the sun had not yet warmed. In a small clearing he picked up another broken branch and began knocking wood-chip "homers," one out to left field, another right over the first baseman's head.

"It's outa here!" He rounded the crumbled log bases and slid in solid on a gopher mound. Scooping a low pitch from the dirt and drilling it hard down to second he shouted, "Tomorrow night, I'm the main man!" He was about to smack another one when he heard Arron calling him back up the hill.

The gnawing and grinding of the chain saw had echoed down the canyon for half an hour before Jason stepped back and drew his arm across his sweaty forehead.

"Man! This thing ain't even budgin'!" He eyed the stubborn ponderosa top to bottom and side to side, analyzing the situation. "Must be fifteen feet around! Maybe I'll hack at the upper side for awhile. That oughta do it."

He made his way up the slope and began chipping at the thick armor of bark with the power blade. In time he had gouged well into the cream-colored inner layers, and the jagged giant finally began to creak with pending motion. Jason straightened up and turned off the saw.

"Gang way, boys! I think she's about to tumble!"

The huge trunk was groaning and the bony branches trembling as Arron and Chipper neared the dirt road that cut across the hillside—just in time to hear the echoing shouts of "Tim-berrr!" Heads were tilted upwards and hands lifted to shade eyes as the boys watched, anticipating a spectacular crash.

Jason was backing uphill away from the tree. He shot a quick glance toward Cade, who had trotted up the road to watch from a safe distance, then turned to check the younger boys he'd left by the truck. He stopped short when he spotted them just fifty feet away, near the road. Panic shot through him like lightning. He cupped his hands and screamed, "Arron! Chipper! Get over by the truck!" But they were oblivious to everything but the teetering tree. Jason began jumping and waving frantically until he finally caught Arron's eye. He motioned wildly toward the truck, hollering for them to run for it.

"Chipper, look out!" Arron called above the crashing noise. His eyes flashed fear as he shot off in the direction of the truck.

Cade's heart lurched as he watched Chipper, frozen like a dazed deer surrounded by firing guns. "Look out! Look out! Go back ! CHIPPER!"

Chipper darted toward him. Huge branches were snapping like twigs and crushing down through the lower limbs. The canyon echoed with the sound of wood cracking against wood. Spindly tree trunks shattered as the hardened deadwood of the ponderosa pushed and knocked its way downward. Like the warning tremor before an earthquake, the mountainside began to shake and rumble. The massive pine was picking up speed, dividing the green sea of trees as it plummeted toward solid ground.

Panic exploded in Jason's chest—Chipper was running directly into the path of the tree. He prayed for a miracle.

The Tree

A loud snap rang out as a dry branch the size of a telephone pole broke loose and lumbered downward. The tree shifted balance and smashed into a ponderosa half its size. It stopped—suspended for several seconds—long enough for Chipper to flash past beneath. Then, with a mighty crack, the dead tree snapped in two and continued it's descent, shaving branches as it fell. There was a final thunderous explosion of dust and debris as the tree hit ground.

"Chipper!"

No answer.

The boys fought their way through the mess of broken branches until they uncovered his legs. Tearing through the tangle of pine boughs, they found him lying face down in the debris.

He wasn't breathing.

2

Unexpected

The road ahead began to blur. Two straight days behind
the wheel was pushing it, even for a trucker. Steve Mangum sat up taller and started whistling, determined to
make it home without a rest stop. He forced his mind to
stay alert by picturing the effect of his surprise appearance.

"Dad! You're home!"

"What's the occasion?"

"Is something wrong?"

Keeping a straight face would be the real trick.

"Yes, I'm afraid there is something wrong. Very wrong." And then the sudden quiet, fallen faces, all heads turned. Oh, he was good at this! "I've been on the road way too long, and it's finally gotten to me."

"What?" They'd all say at once.

"Truckingitis!" Then Sharron would heave a sigh and shake her head like she always did at his silliness while the boys burst out laughing. "And the only known cure is a fishing trip with my boys!"

The happy vision had been repeating in his mind since yesterday. Crazy or not, he was going to push himself to the limit to get a few extra days at home. Chipper had a key Little League game tomorrow night, and this one he was not going to miss. On and on he rolled over the tedious pavement, the incessant thrum of his eighteen-wheeler a backdrop to his focus on the father-son outing. Aspen Mirror Lake would be full of hungry trout. They'd get there by supper time, stir up some Dutch-oven spuds and let 'em simmer while they sank a few lines. A fresh catch on the grill would top it all off. And the guitar—better take the guitar for a round or two of "Oh Where, Oh Where Can My Baby Be."

There it was, finally: Cedar City—Next Three Exits—like a bright green welcome mat on a post. He geared down to steer the rig around the sharp turnoff.

"Scotty! Chipper! Anyone home?"

The words rang empty. Deflated, he took a quick shower and stretched out on the couch to wait for someone to come. It felt good to lie down, to finally let the eyes close, no motor rumbling underneath.

The quiet in the Mangum home was split by the ringing phone next to Steve's ear. For a second he thought he had fallen asleep at the wheel, and he sprang instantly awake and upright.

"Hello?" His voice was only slightly shaky.

"Steve? Is . . . is it you? You're home?" The voice that came across the line was definitely shaky. "It's Evelyn. My mother just called from Duck Creek. The boys were up there cutting wood. There's . . . been an accident. Chipper's hurt."

"What? Where is he now?" Steve was on his feet.

"On his way down . . . to the hospital. Where's Sharron?"

"At the shop, I guess. No one's here. I don't even have a car."

"I'll come and get you. Call Sharron and tell her we're on our way."

Sharron jumped in the car next to her husband, her face drawn in concern. "What did he do this time?" Her effort at sounding calm was a failure.

"Dad said something about a . . . hurt hand."

"Evelyn, I can tell by your face this is worse than stitches on a palm. Tell us what you know."

Evelyn Ashworth kept her eyes on the road. She knew better than to try to keep anything from her best friend, but still hesitated.

"That's all Dad mentioned . . . a hurt hand." It was the truth. But his tone had told her more. He was scared.

Sharron looked so long and hard at Evelyn that Steve tried to ease the tension.

"It's not like we haven't been through this before with Chip. I'll bet he's averaged two emergency room visits a year since he was tiny. Cracked his jaw when he was just a year old. Then there was the broken collarbone, two broken arms, a broken leg. And remember the concussion from the golf ball?"

Sharron managed a slight smile, but it faded as they pulled into the emergency room parking lot.

The receptionist handed them a stack of routine papers, smiling as if emergencies were everyday business. Sharron tried to ignore a nagging headache and force her focus on the forms.

"You'd think I'd be used to this," she told herself. But her stomach was knotted with anxiety. "I wish they'd get here," she said out loud. "I'll feel a lot better when we know what's happened."

Across the hallway in the emergency room nurses were moving quickly about. Code names called out over the intercom. Suddenly Doctor Corry rushed by, speaking into a mobile transmitter as he passed: " . . . unconscious . . . oxygen at 100% per mask . . . prepare to intubate . . . on line to Salt Lake City . . . "

The emergency room doors swung closed and he was gone.

Chipper

"Looks like we're not the only ones with an emergency," Steve whispered to his wife. "Sounds like a stroke or something."

"I hope that doesn't mean Dr. Corry can't help Chip when he comes. I really want our own doctor." As Sharron turned to go inside the waiting room the emergency room door flew open again and the doctor's voice carried above the commotion.

"Critical head wound . . . twelve-year-old boy . . . ten percent chance of survival . . . "

The impact of the doctor's words hit like a shotgun point blank. Sharron grabbed Steve's arm and heard herself gasp. Sirens wailed and everything began whirling. The outside doors burst open. A long blur of white surrounded by cords, bottles, machines, and nurses smeared past them and into the emergency room, leaving them standing alone in the hallway, the haunting words of the doctor still ringing in their ears, " . . . ten percent chance . . . "

Voices . . . calling
So far away
Arron?
I'm falling . . . sinking . . .

3

Live!

Sharron felt a hand on her shoulder. "Mrs. Mangum? I'm DeNean Peterson, Director of Social Services here at the hospital. Can we talk?"

Numb and exhausted, Sharron allowed herself to be led back into the waiting room, barely aware of the friends who were gathering about her. She dropped into a chair

and took a deep breath. She lifted her head and accepted the box of tissues Miss Peterson held out to her.

"Here's an aspirin. Your husband told me you had a headache." Miss Peterson handed her a small paper cup of water. "Where is Mr. Mangum now?"

"He went with our Bishop to . . . give Chipper a blessing." Sharron swallowed the aspirin. She lifted her eyes and looked hard into the face of Miss Peterson before more words came. When they did, they were pleading, earnest. "He's got to live! My son . . . they said he had just a ten percent chance!" Miss Peterson took Sharron's hand.

"Sharron, look around the room. These people are pulling for you, and your son. This kind of strength and support brings about miracles. I've seen it happen. Don't let any statistic drag down your hope. We don't know for sure right now what your son's situation is. They'll take him into x-ray, then after Dr. Corry has had a chance to examine him, he'll talk with you and your husband. That will help a lot."

As Miss Peterson left, a new wave of panic hit. Sharron realized she must soon deal with the raw truth. Not knowing held a degree of comfort. She looked at the phone book that Miss Peterson had left for her, grateful for a moment's distraction.

"My kids. I should call my kids."

Evelyn was at her side. This time her husband, Ash, was with her.

"We called them," he assured her. "They're on their way."

Live!

Sharron loosened her grip on the box of tissues she had been clinging to and pulled out a handful. The wad of Kleenex seemed to give her permission to release the knot of emotion that had settled tight in her chest. She bent forward and put her face in her hands. Ash started toward her, paused.

"Let her cry," Evelyn whispered.

Several minutes passed before Sharron raised her head and took a deep breath. Evelyn put an arm around her. They didn't need words. Ash checked his watch and walked over to an empty seat. Sharron met his gaze.

"Will it be OK if Chipper misses a few games?" The words seemed strange, even to Sharron. Ash threw an uncertain glance at his wife before answering.

"Sure. Sure."

A young boy in a baseball cap hesitated at the door. Sharron started forward.

"Chipper?"

The boy's eyes darted around the room.

Evelyn turned and saw her son Arron in the doorway. His eyes were wide, his face pale and smudged, his hands and clothes covered with blood. She rushed to his side.

Arron looked across the room at Sharron, then dropped his eyes to the floor. His breath came in jerks as he attempted to speak.

"The tree . . . it fell wrong. Chipper . . . he . . . he was trying to get away, but . . . we thought he was . . . dead!"

A sudden shudder shook his small frame, and tears began to spill down his dirty cheeks. He buried his face in his hands and turned to his mom. Evelyn pulled him close.

"It's OK, Arron. It's OK. You did all you could." He let his mom hold and rock him for several minutes, until his trembling stopped.

Sharron watched the scene with new pain, wanting to say something that would heal the hurt in his face. "You're a good friend, Arron." It didn't seem like enough, but it was all that would come.

"Sharron?" Steve was back. "Dr. Corry can talk to us now."

The only light in the x-ray room came from a small screen on the wall where Dr. Corry was clipping up exposures of Chipper's skull. The room felt cold, and Steve put his arm around Sharron as they crossed the floor. Dr. Corry's voice was quiet but direct.

"These shadowy areas show where Chipper's skull was cracked. As you can see, he has major fractures running from ear to ear and from crown to forehead. Right here," he pointed to a darker area about the size of a baseball, "the bone is completely shattered. Gone."

"No!" Sharron clasped a hand to her mouth and looked at Steve, who was shaking his head in disbelief.

"In all honesty"—Dr. Corry was almost whispering —"I'm amazed that Chipper made it down the mountain alive."

There was a moment of silence before Steve spoke, his voice strangely controlled. "What happens next?"

"The next few hours are extremely critical. Chipper's alive right now only because he's on a total life-support system. He needs brain surgery, but we're not equipped to do it here. I've been in contact with Dr. Lynn Wright at

Primary Children's Medical Center in Salt Lake City. She's already dispatched a Life Flight plane. Their brain trauma team is one of the best. He'll be transported within the hour." Dr. Corry searched their faces. "Do you have any questions?"

"Questions!" Sharron thought. Unspeakable questions were burning through her. "Will my son ever be the same again? Will he throw a ball, or even walk again? Talk again?" But no words came. It was as if speaking them would make her fears more real.

"Can we go with him on the flight? I think he needs us with him." Steve's words sliced into Sharron's thoughts.

Dr. Corry hesitated only a moment. "I'm sure I can arrange that," he assured. "Now, if you're ready, I'll take you in to see him."

"Dr. Corry?" Sharron stopped, and the doctor turned. "I need to know what he's feeling. Does he know . . . anything that's going on? Is he in pain?"

"No, I don't think he can feel any pain. He's unconscious and under a lot of medication. I doubt he's aware of much. Consciously, anyway."

Sharron made her feet push forward then paused several feet from the bed, drawing from the depths of her soul to find strength to deal with what she saw.

Chipper lay motionless on a padded table in the middle of the room, his face as white as the walls around him. His head was horribly swollen. Blood was draining from his nose and both ears and Sharron had to force her eyes to keep focusing. His blond hair looked brown, matted with blood and dirt. Nurses were swabbing blood and debris from a gaping gash down his left side. His Levi's had been cut away, revealing more lacerations on his left leg. His left hand was mangled, still oozing blood. Tubes, cords and machines surrounded him, nurses stationed at each post. Air was being pumped into his lungs, fluids drained through needles into his veins.

Sharron's head was spinning.

"We've put him in a state of hypothermia, what you might call a medicated deep freeze," the doctor was saying. "This will preserve his energy and help keep him alive until we get him to surgery. He may be able to hear you subconsciously. Go ahead and talk to him."

Standing by the bedside, Steve turned to Sharron, still several feet away. Her eyes were fixed on Chipper, her face registering the struggle going on inside. Slowly she walked to the bedside, took her son's hand and held it close. It was alarmingly stiff and cold. Her eyes shot to the doctor's, seeking reassurance, which he gave with a silent nod.

"Chipper? Can you hear me?" Sharron spoke with effort, determined to make him feel her there, know she was with him. "It's Mum. I'm here, Son. You're going to be all right. Hang on, Chipper. We're taking care of you. We love you." Her voice broke and faltered. Steve leaned in closer and took over.

"You can pull through this, Chipper." With his mouth right by Chipper's ear, he whispered, "Live, Son. Live!"

DeNean Peterson spoke from the doorway. "Mr. and Mrs. Mangum, your children are here."

Steve and Sharron exchanged glances, and Steve nodded to Miss Peterson. If he had been more certain they would see their brother again, he might not have allowed them in the room.

Terie Mangum walked forward, followed more hesitantly by her younger brother Scotty and her older sister Karie. She stepped up to the table and laid her hand on her little brother's arm.

"Oh, Chipper!" Her lips trembled and she tightened them, blinking. "Don't worry, you'll be OK. Won't he, Dad?" Her eyes found her father.

"If anyone can pull through this, he can." Steve made his voice optimistic and even managed a smile. He turned to Scotty and Karie, still barely inside the doorway. "It's OK kids. Come on in."

Karie stood in a daze behind her sister. She picked up on her father's words of encouragement.

"Yes, he can pull through this. He'll be OK. Everything will be all right." Talking more to herself than anyone else, she repeated the same words again, then looked for the first time at her mother and dad. "Don't worry. He's going to be all right," she said again, this time for them.

Sixteen-year-old Scott was struggling to be strong. His face was tight with pain and worry, his eyes working to blink back tears. He swallowed hard and shook his head as he stood over his brother. His first attempt to speak ended in a muffled sob. He didn't try again for a while. He wiped at his eyes with the back of his hand and drew in a long breath, forcing control in his voice.

"Will they keep him here?"

"No, they'll have to Life Flight him to Salt Lake. Mum and I will go with him."

Chipper

"Can we go?"

"It would be best if you waited here until morning. We'll call and let you know . . . whatever happens."

"Don't worry, Mum, Dad," Terie stepped up and began taking the situation in hand, as she always did in a crisis. "We'll go home and get some things together for you and let people know what's happened. Then we'll drive up the minute we hear from you."

As the family filed into the hallway, they were encircled by friends. A neighbor pushed through the crowd and pressed a key into Steve's hand.

"It's to our Townhouse in Salt Lake. It's yours for as long as you need it."

Steve grasped his hand thankfully and pushed on down the hallway to keep up with his wife and the stretcher carrying his son.

Air . . .
Swooshing
Throbbing shadows
Moving . . . still . . . moving . . . and still
Swirling whispers of sound

"Live, Son . . . Live!"

4

Sparks of Hope

Things happened fast from the moment the airplane rolled to a stop. An ambulance waited on the runway, lights flashing. Medical personnel darted forward, lifting the stretcher from airplane to ambulance in a matter of seconds. Steve and Sharron rushed behind. The siren wailed as they laced their way down the highway, sped past stopped traffic, bolted through red-lighted intersections.

Steve looked at Sharron, who was holding onto the seat with both hands. "It's too bad Chipper won't remember this ride. He'd love it."

"I'll tell him all about it," Sharron gulped.

The scramble of activity increased as they pulled to the back of a white brick building and up a ramp marked:
PRIMARY CHILDREN'S MEDICAL CENTER
EMERGENCY ENTRANCE

After infinite minutes of rushing, pushing, pulling, transferring, rehooking, Chipper once again lay on a brightly lit emergency room table. The flurry and scrambling quieted. A circle of robed and masked doctors and nurses exchanged terse commands, working with teamlike efficiency. Steve and Sharron found themselves standing in a corner of the emergency room. Above them on the wall a clock ticked the seconds by, a visible reminder that precious time was passing. Sharron found herself clutching Steve's arm, feeling like a piece of equipment stored in the shadows awaiting its time of need, for the moment, useless.

"Your boy is in good hands." They jumped at the sound of the voice behind them.

"I'm sorry. I didn't mean to startle you. I'm Dr. Faulkner, one of the neurological specialists."

The firm handshake pulled the two from the corner.

"I know you would like to stay with your son, but we need to have you check in at the front desk and sign some

forms. I want to introduce you to some staff social workers, too. They'll be a lot of help."

Busying himself with the papers, Steve found his tension easing a little. It felt better to be doing something. As
he signed his name and passed the clipboard to his wife he
could sense her discomfort in being away from Chipper.

He took her hand and they started back toward the
emergency room. Hearing a child's voice cry out, they
made a dash for the door. Just as they were about to burst
in, a hand reached out and caught Steve's shoulder.
"Wait—it's not your son. They've taken him for a CAT
scan. Then he'll go right into surgery." Dr. Faulkner's voice
was calm and matter-of-fact. "Please, come with me."

The doctor led them to a private waiting room, ac-
quainting them with the layout of the hospital on the way.
He sat with them for several minutes, giving instructions
and answering questions.

The door swung open. Sharron started to her feet.

"Please, don't get up." The stocky man in green surgical
scrubs and cap gestured for them to stay seated. "I'm Dr.
Walker. I'll be heading the surgical team. Before we begin, I
want to talk to you about the findings of our initial examination. I'm not sure how much you already know, so I'll
just start at the beginning. Most of the damage to your
son's skull is on the left side, where it's shattered. Splinters
of bone and wood are lodged in the brain itself. He's missing a considerable amount of skull, and more critically,
brain tissue. He has sustained a number of other injuries,
including a major problem with his spleen. But the brain

swelling is our primary concern at this point." When the doctor paused, Steve jumped in.

"Will he . . . make it?"

The hesitation in the air was painful, and Steve and Sharron found themselves looking intently at each other, afraid to hear Dr. Walker's words when they finally came.

"Some things can't be determined until we get into surgery and can actually see the extent of the damage." As his eyes met theirs, he could plainly read they wanted more. That look was too familiar. Even after all these years in practice, it tore at his heart and reminded him of his limitations. "I would guess . . . he has a thirty percent chance of surviving the surgery. As for how much function he'll be left with, that's more difficult to determine. We'll do our best."

In the heavy silence that hung in the room after the doctor left, Sharron found herself avoiding the anxious gaze of her husband. She stared at the clock until its tedious ticking made her head pound. She searched the room and found herself focusing on meaningless details: the fleck of green in the peach carpet, the seams in the pastel wallpaper. She looked for windows. Where were the windows? The room needed windows, somewhere to look out, to allow thoughts to escape from her throbbing head and float to some safe, far-off place.

"A thirty percent chance is better than ten." Steve's words forced her to look at him.

She nodded, thinking she should say something, but lacking the energy. She stood and walked over to the small fridge. Hand trembling, she reached inside for a can of

Sprite, knowing she wouldn't drink it. She sank back into her chair and stared blankly ahead for several minutes, hands cupped around the icy can, until a shudder shook her whole body. The clock on the wall came back into focus. It was past midnight. Again she tore her gaze from it, glancing at her husband. His head was back and his eyes were closed, but his expression was anything but restful. His hair was tousled, his face lined with worry. He looked exhausted, and no wonder. Sharron counted the hours since he had last slept: forty-two.

"CODE BLUE! CODE BLUE!"

The piercing tones of the intercom jerked Steve's eyes wide open.

"What's that?"

"I don't know. I'll step out in the hall and see if I can find out. You need to get some rest."

Sharron found herself standing outside the surgery room doors. She leaned on the doorframe. It felt cool on her pounding forehead. Part of her desperately wished to know what was going on behind those doors; another part shrunk at the thought.

The halls were quiet, almost eerie. A lonely feeling crept over her, and she had a sudden urge to call home.

"Evelyn?" I didn't expect you to answer."

"Oh, Sharron! It's you. I told the kids to get some rest while I listened for the phone. Let me go wake them."

"No, let them sleep. We haven't got anything new to report. I . . . just needed to call."

"I'm so glad you did. What's happening up there?"

"Chipper's in surgery. Over four hours now. It'll take most of the night, I guess."

Evelyn sighed. "Jason is beside himself, Sharron. He's taking this whole thing so hard."

"I hope he's not blaming himself." The line went silent. Evelyn tried to speak but couldn't. Jason wasn't the only one blaming himself and they both knew it. Finally Sharron spoke.

"We're not looking for blame Ev, we're looking for miracles. Let's hope we find some."

"We already have." Evelyn was grateful to focus on something less painful. "Aaron keeps talking about how Cade lifted that huge branch off Chipper like Superman. It's a miracle those boys got him off the mountain so quickly. And Sharron, he's alive. That's the biggest miracle of all."

Cold black
Torn by spears
Sparks
Burning red . . . blue
Flashing yellow
Swirling down
A black funnel . . .
No . . . no!

5

Call Me Chipper

It was almost 2:00 in the morning when the door opened again. After eight hours in surgery, Dr. Walker and his assistants came into the waiting room. Face masks hung limp around their necks and lines of weariness and strain creased their eyes.

"Christopher's surgery went remarkably well. We cleaned out the fragments and debris, meshed and wired the left side of his skull together. We've done all we can for now." After a deep breath, Dr. Walker continued. "As we had feared, there is a substantial amount of actual brain tissue missing or damaged."

"So what does that mean for Chipper?" Sharron could wait no longer to ask the question she had been mulling for so long. Dr. Walker shifted his weight.

"The damaged areas of his brain control speech, reasoning, learning, memory . . . and the motor skills for the right side of his body. I'm afraid his ability levels will be severely affected in all these areas. Exactly how debilitating Christopher's injuries are, we can only guess at this point. His prognosis can only be determined a day at a time by watching his behavior, if—when he regains consciousness."

Steve cleared his dry throat. "Are we still looking at a thirty percent chance?"

"We're at a critical point right now, Mr. Mangum. It's natural for you to want specifics, but it's not that easy. I can say this much; if your son lives the next forty-eight hours free of infection and complication, he will have a chance of surviving."

A burdened silence hung in the air. Dr. Walker looked at his assistants, giving them a chance to speak.

"There are all kinds of complicating factors with brain trauma," Dr. Faulkner began. "Your boy has suffered a lot of bruising, which creates the risk of blood clots. His brain has been contaminated with outside elements, which means a high risk of infection that his body may not be able to handle. But this child has a strong constitution. He's a tenacious little guy. We could feel him fighting for all he's worth. That gives Christopher a real advantage, I assure you."

"Chipper," Steve said.

"Pardon?"

"We call him Chipper," Steve repeated.

"Oh. Chipper. It fits. Now, can we answer any more questions before we go?"

Sharron struggled to gather the thoughts whirling in her mind and put them in question form. Her listeners were patient. "Where do we come in? I mean, I want to do something to help my son. I don't think I can spend another minute in a waiting room, not knowing what is going on, not being with him . . . "

Dr. Walker stepped closer to Sharron and placed his hand on her shoulder. "You can go to your son very soon, Mrs. Mangum. But I'm afraid you are in for a lot more waiting. Maybe it will be a bit easier when you are by his side. I hope so. You can count on days, maybe even weeks or months of waiting. Christopher–Chipper has a real challenge ahead. As for how you can help: let me assure you your role is vital. It has been my experience that no amount of medication or doctoring can compare with love. I believe that Chipper can hear you, or at least sense your presence. Talk to him. A lot. Encourage him, tell him stories, sing to him, re-live his past with him. Just let him know you're there."

Sharron wept as she listened, and Steve drew her close to him, laboring to control his own emotions.

Chipper

"Can we go to him now?"

"He will be back in the ICU and ready to have you join him in about thirty minutes."

But they could not wait thirty minutes. After watching the clock for fifteen, Steve grabbed Sharron's hand.

"We're going in!"

The words "Intensive Care Unit" glared like a warning across the double doors. Steve pushed through and led his wife into the semi-darkness. They tiptoed between beds divided by white curtains and surrounded by countless machines that ticked different rhythms and blinked shades of cold green light in the shadows.

"Here!" Sharron whispered, coming to a halt at the foot of one of the beds. The boy in bed lay still, his head wrapped in a spiral of bandages. Tubes were inserted into both arms and down his throat.

"Chipper?" Steve bent over him in the darkness. Sharron reached out to touch his leg. A gasp escaped her throat.

"What?" Steve whirled in alarm.

"His . . . his leg!" Sharron stammered. Steve looked down at the flat, smooth space on the bed where the left leg should have been. He grabbed for his wife, who was steadying herself, both hands clutching the side-bar of the bed, eyes squeezed shut.

A nurse was suddenly at their side. "Are you the Thompsons?"

"Thompsons? No, we're the Mangums," Steve answered feebly.

"Oh, this is Tug Thompson. Your son's bed is down there, where you see the lights." She pointed to a bed surrounded by nurses farther down the row. Sharron's sigh of relief was as audible as her gasp had been. The nurse put an arm around her.

"I'm Paula, the head nurse tonight." Her young face emitted confidence and vitality. Though Sharron's hand was still trembling, Paula's grasp was firm and competent.

"Steady, Mom. It's OK. Let's go find Christopher."

Another nurse joined them.

"This is Tina," Paula said as they moved toward the right bed. "Christopher may not have a room of his own, but he has his own private nurse, and she's the greatest." Paula chattered on in low and easy tones that sounded unaffected by the circumstances.

"I wish we could tell you how long your son will be our guest here, but that's always so uncertain. We like to hang on to them, we get so attached to these kids." As they approached his bed, Sharron felt her fears tightening with every step. The nurse's words passed like mist through her mind; she wasn't really hearing them. " . . . going to be great friends with this guy before we're through. Aren't we, Christopher?"

The nurse stepped aside and pulled back the curtain to let Steve and Sharron in close. Sharron reached out impulsively and touched her son's leg. She looked him over, head to toe, taking everything in, silently shaking her head in disbelief. The child she saw before her didn't look any more like her son than the first boy they had seen. His face was unrecognizable, so swollen it was almost impossible to make out features. His eyes were nothing more than two slits buried in the swollen flesh. His gray-white skin was splotched with every shade of purple and red imaginable. His head was not bandaged. Half-inch staples held the swollen skin together and a two-inch bolt protruded from the left side of his skull. There were more tubes and needles, this time in his nose, in the top of his head, in his side, as well as several in his arms and legs. Paula began talking again, her quiet voice more serious now.

"Don't let the swelling and bruises alarm you. That's normal. The bolt in his head is to drain the fluids and relieve the pressure as much as possible. This tube is irrigating his spleen. We hope we can save it. That surgery, as well as a few on his hand and leg, will have to wait until he's a little stronger. This tube is supplying blood. His tank was pretty low by the time we got him. The machine over there"–she pointed to the head of his bed–"is breathing for him. He can't do much on his own right now. Can you, Christopher?" She patted his shoulder gently. It was Steve who broke the silence that followed.

"We call him Chipper."

"Oh, Chipper, huh? Well, we can't expect him to answer us if we aren't calling him by the right name." Tearing a page from her clipboard, she wrote in big bold letters "CALL ME CHIPPER" and taped it securely to the head of his bed.

"There you go. Chipper it is."

Reaching arms
Who's there?
Circling shadows

Call Me Chipper

Pulling, pressing
Click . . . clicking
A dream
Nightmare
Wake up, wake up!

" . . . call him Chipper."

Chipper?

6

Cocoon

Morning was slow coming. Sharron jumped when Tina pushed open the curtain around Chipper's bed.

"Haven't you gone to sleep yet?" The nurse stooped to review the chart hanging at the foot of Chipper's bed. "It's barely 5:00 A.M. I thought only nurses and other wandering phantoms were up at this hour." When Sharron didn't respond, Tina turned to her.

"Are you OK, Mom?"

"The swelling is worse—I can't even see his ears!" Speaking the words out loud broke her dam of resistance and the tears started again. Tina came to her side.

"The hardest thing for a mother to do is watch her child suffer and not be able to do anything about it. I wish I had a magic formula I could give you that would make this ordeal easier. Two things might help a little," she said. "First, this swelling, however bizarre it may appear, is expected, and it will peak soon. Second, Chipper isn't feeling any pain. Let me show you." Tina led Sharron to one of the monitors at the head of the bed. "This baby is measuring and recording some important statistics. We can look at it and know instantly if Chipper is hurting. We don't know if he can even feel pain while in a coma, but we would never chance it. We adjust his medication as if he could. It's our job to keep this little guy comfortable, and we're good at what we do." Tina turned a caring smile toward Sharron. "Now Mom, does that help?"

Sharron nodded, feeling like a frightened child herself.

"How would you like to help with Chipper's rubdown a little later? We can't put him in the tub for a few days, so we give him a bit of a bath right here. It helps his circulation and hopefully helps stimulate some response."

Sharron brightened. "I'd love that. It would feel so good to do something . . . anything." Her eyes were on her son, lying so still. "I just want him to know I'm here."

"I think he knows." Tina gave Sharron's shoulder a squeeze before reaching to pull open the curtain. A shaft of rosy sunlight filtered over the bed. "Now that's a sunrise! I suggest you take advantage of our exclusive front row seat." She turned a chair to face the window, gave the pillow in it a pat, and left to attend to the next patient. Sharron stepped closer to the window.

The mountains stretched tall to block the rising sun but the climbing rays spread warming fingers between the pink clouds. The light brightened until the sun's golden palm appeared, pouring light into the valley below. It felt good to Sharron to let some thoughts wander outside, to mingle with the hope and freshness of a new day.

Sharron leaned to examine an empty gray cocoon that clung tentatively to a budding twig by the window. What fuzzy little creature had spun itself into that dark chamber to work its mysterious metamorphosis? She watched the dried chrysalis teeter in the breeze for a few moments, pondering.

"Sharron?"

"Oh, Steve. I didn't hear you come in."

"I noticed. What are you thinking about in that trance?"

"Cocoons."

"What?"

"Cocoons. See?" Steve stepped closer to the window and Sharron pointed out her discovery. "It's empty now. The little fellow has flown away." Sharron turned to look at her son. "I wonder what changes will have occurred when Chipper comes out of his cocoon. And I wonder if I can love the butterfly without missing the caterpillar."

Tina was back, this time with a doctor at her side.

"Have you two met Dr. Vernon?"

"Yes. He was here most of the night." Steve stood to shake his hand. "Don't you guys ever sleep?"

Dr. Vernon got right to business. "I'm glad you're both here. We want to work at getting a response this morning. It's time for Chipper to wake up."

"You expect a response so soon?"

"When I say 'response,' I don't mean words." Dr. Vernon moved to examine the red scribbles on a scroll coming from one of the monitors. "I want you to talk to Chipper. Talk to him as if he could hear you."

Sharron and Steve positioned themselves on either side of the bed then looked at each other. Leaning forward, close to Chipper's ear, Sharron spoke first.

"Chipper. Chipper, it's Mum. Wake up, Honey. It's morning. Time to wake up." She paused. Chipper didn't move.

"I'm here too, Son. How are you feeling this morning? Can you open your eyes? Can you hear me, Chip?" Steve stood upright and looked at the doctor, who was intently watching the monitor.

"Keep at it," he whispered.

Encouraged, they continued.

"Chipper, we want you to wake up now. Please wake up, Son."

"Try hard, Chipper. Try as hard as you did when you hit that homer last Saturday. You can do it. We know you can do it."

This time Steve and Sharron watched the monitor too. There was a fleck of change in the series of lines, a tiny jump in the needle.

"He can hear us!" Steve breathed out the words, hardly daring to believe them.

"I think he can," Dr. Vernon said matter-of-factly. He circled the response on the printout, with the nurse beaming over his shoulder. "It's hard to tell how much of his response is subconscious, but this is definitely a positive sign." He put his pen back in his coat pocket and looked up. "Dr. Walker will want to see this. Keep talking to him. We don't want to tire him out, but the sooner he is out of this coma, the better his chances for improvement."

Steve watched the doctor turn and shuffle off to the next station, both shoes untied. "I'm not entirely sure what happened there, but it sure seemed like a step in the right direction."

Sharron took his arm. "I think our butterfly wants to try out his new wings."

It was close to noon when the kids arrived from home. Tina tapped Sharron and told her her children were in the family waiting room. She snapped a Polaroid picture of Chipper to help prepare them for the shock of seeing their brother.

"Do you want me to show this to them, or would you like to do it?"

Sharron took the picture. "Will you come with me?"

Karie, Terie, and Scott crowded around the picture. They stood there in a silent line, staring at the photo in disbelief. Finally, Terie stepped back and reached for her purse.

"I want to show you what my little brother really looks like," she told the nurse. Tina took the school picture and looked into the face of an All-American kid. Sandy blond hair, a sprinkle of freckles, and an unmistakable spark of mischief in his green eyes.

"Can we keep this a while?" she asked Terie. "No one will want to miss this cute mug."

She led the group back up the hallway and through the ICU doors and taped the picture to the sign that said "CALL ME CHIPPER."

Sharron and Steve sat in the cafeteria. Terie had insisted they take a break and it had felt good to finally take a shower and put on some clean clothes after two long nights.

"They're strong, those kids of ours," Steve was saying. "I really thought it might be more than they could handle."

"They're awesome, as Chipper would say," Sharron answered, standing to empty her lunch tray.

"Don't you want to relax a minute? The kids can sit with him." Sharron sat back down, but was so fidgety that Steve laughed. "All right, mother hen, let's get back to your chicks."

At first it alarmed Sharron to see Scotty running down the hall toward them, but the wide grin on his face put her heart to rest.

"Mum! Dad! The nurse wants you, quick. She thinks Chipper is trying to wake up!"

Chipper

The few feet down the hall stretched long, like a distant mirage. Scotty was running sideways, breathlessly explaining what had happened.

"I was trying to get him to pull my finger, and his eyelids moved! You should have seen how excited the nurse got. She told me to get you guys up there—fast!"

When they finally reached Chipper's bed, Dr. Walker was already there. Scotty pushed by him to his brother's side. Taking up Chip's hand, he forced his voice to be calm.

"Chipper, it's me again. I got Mum and Dad here now. Show them what you can do, huh Bro? Pull my finger." Scotty was so excited he could hardly stand still. His eyes jumped from the monitor to Chipper's face and back again. "You can do it, Chip. I know you can!"

Again the red lines jogged on the page, and Chipper's eyelids fluttered briefly. Steve bent close.

"That's it, Chipper boy! Open your eyes! Keep at it!" Steve was intent, straining to see any flicker or change. But this time, there was nothing. He kept trying, totally absorbed, until Dr. Walker reached out and touched him.

"It will come. He's working at it. Let's give him a little more time."

Heavy black blankets
Holding me
Tangled ropes
Tight, pinching

"Wake up, Chipper . . . "

Cocoon

Shots of light
Twisting, blurring
Caught . . . stuck!

"Chipper, pull!"

Help me.
Pull me out!

7

Coming and Going

The next two days and nights fused into one long vigil. Steve and Sharron took turns watching the lines and lights on Chipper's monitors, anxiously waiting, hour upon hour. Any jump in graphing needle or change in flashing light prompted a quick nurse call.

"Is it a sign he's awake?"

"No. But it's a sign he's alive," Tina responded, grinning.

"Why is it taking so long?" Sharron sighed, her cheek resting against the side-bar of the bed. "Nothing seems to get through to him at all. We talk to him, sing to him, read to him, touch him . . . and this swelling. When will it stop?"

Tina came to her side.

"It's a slow process, Sharron. The changes are gradual, sometimes hardly noticeable. It's not like Chipper is going to suddenly open his eyes and be out of the coma. "That just happens in the movies. His eyes will flutter, sometimes even open for a while, but that won't necessarily mean he's conscious. We call this a 'semi-comatose state.' It's an in-and-out sort of thing, coming and going, you might say, until he finally comes to stay."

Sharron pondered the last words. She raised her head. "Dr. Vernon said the sooner he regains consciousness, the better his chances of progressing. I just wonder what he will be like when he does come . . . to stay."

"That's the question we're all asking. But none of us can answer yet, Mom. We can only wait and see."

A team of medical attendants burst in wheeling a bed. Within the tangles of wires and tubes lay a tiny dark-haired baby. Her mother followed, wide eyes darting around the room.

"Oh, there's the Navajo child." Tina started off. "Her mother doesn't understand any English. She could probably use a friend."

The Indian woman sobbed in the shadows as the nurses settled the child in her station. When attempts were made to communicate or comfort the mother, she would shake her head in quick movements that said, "I do not understand."

Sharron turned from the scene to the window. The valley below teemed with morning motion, cars thick on the crisscrossing streets. People honking horns, swerving, rushing on, with no clue of what was happening behind the sturdy walls of the hospital. No idea of how lives were being thrown into whirlpools of suffering, life and death suddenly immediate.

When Sharron turned back, the woman was sitting alone. Sharron poured juice in a cup and walked over to her. She offered the juice, but the woman just stared up at her.

Sharron attempted to communicate. "I'm sorry. Your baby. I hope she will be OK. My son is very sick, too," she gestured toward Chipper. The woman's glazed expression did not change. After Sharron left her, she began weeping and rocking back and forth, mumbling to herself and cooing to her baby.

Walking in, Steve felt the heaviness in the air. He offered Sharron some toast and sat beside her. They were talking softly when an alarm sounded across the room, bringing the nurses and doctors running to the baby's side. Sharron jumped to her feet, and might have run over herself to help, had Steve not taken her hand. The two of them watched helplessly as the attendants rushed here and there, giving vital commands, exchanging anxious looks. The mother stood by, her eyes flashing fear and alarm.

The baby could not be revived.

The haunting wail of the grieving mother filled the ICU chambers. Steve put his arm around Sharron, holding tight as they watched a nurse lead the stricken woman from the room, her grief clear and piercing in any language. It was a disquieting moment for Terie and Scotty to enter to tell their parents goodbye. The family circled Chipper's bed for a prayer. They held hands in silence for a long time, looking at Chipper, at each other, so aware of the fragile balance of life and their own vulnerability. Each knew that no matter what happened, the Mangum family would never be the same.

It was late afternoon when Paula came with the lotion for Chipper's bath and rubdown. Sharron joined her at the bedside. The two women gently washed between Chipper's wounds, neither of them speaking for several minutes.

"Tell me more about him," Paula asked quietly.

Sharron breathed a deep sigh and let her thoughts stroll through memories that seemed years past.

"He loves music," she began. "He plays the drums in the school band—and takes bagpipe lessons." A slight smile touched her lips.

"Bagpipes? That's got to be a first around here. I'm going to insist on a concert!" Paula's delight was genuine. "Tell me more."

"He has a dog named Buddy. His best friend, Arron, is taking care of him while we're here. Evelyn says the dog just mopes around their house all day. He hasn't been separated from Chipper like this before. Neither has Arron, for that matter. The two boys have grown up together. We tell them they're like a pair of tennis shoes, always on the run and just a step away from each other.

"Arron rode with Chipper in the truck after the accident. All the way down that mountain. He held his own shirt to Chipper's bleeding head . . . " She paused and gazed into space. "I worry how something like that could affect such a young boy."

"He sounds like a real hero. The kind of friend Chipper will need when he gets home." Paula's eyes shone with concern. Sharron realized Paula was waiting for her to continue.

"Chipper loves sports. He lives and breathes baseball—and he's good! This season, Ash, his coach, says he's a shoo-in as catcher for the all-star team. It'll be such a thrill for him." Sharron caught herself. "Or at least, it would have been."

"Well, our Chipper's in for adventures of a new dimension now." Paula spoke as if she shared the motherhood of the boy whose leg she gently rubbed. There was a depth of knowing in her touch, her eyes.

After dinner, activity picked up again in the ICU. Dr. Vernon was setting up monitors once more by the bed across from the Mangums. He attended to several details, then stepped over to where Steve and Sharron sat.

"We have a five-year-old girl coming in from your hometown. Wendy Wood. Do you know her?"

Steve and Sharron exchanged glances before Steve spoke.

"Don't recognize the name. What happened?"

"She was thrown from a runaway horse. She hit the ground head first and lost consciousness immediately. Right now her folks are in a real state of shock and panic. You know how that feels, huh?" The doctor gave Sharron's arm a squeeze before hurrying off.

Within minutes, they wheeled Wendy into the room. Her parents were close by her, her mother clutching a stuffed reindeer playing Christmas music. Sharron immediately recognized the mother's face.

"I've seen her before. She works at Albertsons," she whispered to Steve.

The little girl's condition was obviously critical. Her head was swollen even beyond what they had seen with Chipper. She had no open wound, so a valve had been inserted into her skull to relieve the pressure. The doctors and nurses scurried around the bed for almost an hour before things settled down enough for Steve and Sharron to walk over and introduce themselves to Matt and Marilyn Wood. They talked briefly, the time not right for much discussion. Sharron's lack of sleep was catching up to her, leaving her emotions too close to the surface to be of much comfort. Steve suggested she take a break, and she headed for the parents' room. He settled back into the chair at Chipper's bedside, watching the blinking lights of the monitors, until his own eyes were lulled closed.

A buzzing alarm startled him from his doze. Shooting out of his chair, he stood looking across the aisle to where the dreaded sound had come from before. As his mind cleared he realized the alarm was not coming from across the room. It was screaming from behind him—from Chipper's monitor! By this time doctors and nurses were running to Chipper's bedside.

Terror gripped Steve as he stepped back out of the way, glaring at the flat lines on the monitor above Chipper's head, barely able to breathe. His eyes darted from monitor to nurse to doctor to Chipper. Finally the terrifying straight lines began to bend and peak until they returned to the normal scribble.

"He's not about to give in!" Paula said.

She and the others returned to what they were doing as if saving a life were routine. Still shaking, Steve collapsed into his chair, too drained even to ask any questions. When Sharron came up to take her turn at the bedside, Steve was staring ahead, misty eyed.

"Steve? Steve, are you OK.?"

He stared ahead as he spoke. "He was gone. It wasn't long, but he was gone."

"What are you talking about?"

He met her eyes. "I felt it, Sharron. He left us for a moment. But he came back."

"What are you saying?" Sharron's voice was rising in alarm.

But Steve's remained perfectly calm. "I think," he arose and took both Sharron's hands. "I think if he were going to die, he would have. Just now. But he didn't. He's still here. The time has passed, and he is still with us. He's going to make it, Sharron." He bent over Chipper, squeezing his cold hand. "You *are* going to make it, aren't you, Chipper."

Coming and Going

Rubbing . . . licking
Buddy?
Running
In the sunlight
Wait!
I want to come
Warm bright light . . .

Ringing
Loud . . . hard
Screaming!
Pulling me . . . back

"You *are* going to make it, aren't you Chipper."

8

Day Five and Counting

The morning of June 10 dawned brighter. Paula came to the parents' room around 7:00 A.M. with good news: The swelling had peaked in the night and Chipper's temperature was nearly normal.

Steve and Sharron hurried back to ICU. They found Chipper churning in his bed like he was having a bad dream. Tina was there, preparing him to be moved.

"Good morning, Mom and Dad. We're getting ready for a little trip to surgery, have you heard? Dr. Walker says we can go ahead and stitch up some of those other war wounds."

Sharron didn't know if she should be excited or frightened.

"Are you sure he's ready for this? Shouldn't we give him a little more time?"

"Doctor's orders, Mom. I'm not arguing with experience. He'll be a few hours, so I brought you a little reading material to keep you busy. Keep track of any questions. We'll be back."

A couple of orderlies whisked Chipper, bed and all, down the hall to surgery. With a quick sweep Steve grabbed the papers and the two of them followed as far as the waiting room. Steve settled himself into a chair, but Sharron hesitated at the door.

"When this ordeal is over, I don't think I'll ever go into another waiting room," she sighed.

"There are worse things than waiting," he said, watching his wife pace the floor. "Here, try to relax a minute and read over some of this with me."

He handed Sharron a pamphlet as she took a seat and forced her focus on the first page. It described the typical behavioral stages of brain injured patients. Words like *agitation, confusion, bizarre, aggression* and *robot-like* glared from the paper. Sharron shuddered at the thought of her son fitting any of these terms. Even more frightening was the possibility that each stage could take a long time to overcome, or worse, could be as far as Chipper would progress.

Sharron leaned back and closed her eyes, the papers limp in her lap. "I just can't comprehend all this."

"Then don't try right now." Steve stood up. "Let's go celebrate."

Her eyes opened. "Celebrate?"

"Yes. Celebrate the good things. Chipper has made some real strides." Steve took the papers from Sharron's hands, folded them and stuffed them in his pocket. "Let's take this one step at a time, OK? Today Chipper got on base, and I've never seen a game yet where he was content to stop at first. Or where you weren't in the stands cheering him on." He pulled Sharron to her feet.

Many of the faces in the cafeteria were familiar. Some the Mangums had spoken with and others they had just seen in halls and waiting rooms. Seated at a table near the door were the parents of the other two children from Southern Utah.

"We've heard your good news," Julie Thompson called out.

"Chipper's showing improvement, huh?" Matt Wood pulled a couple of chairs over and Steve and Sharron set their trays down. "That's great!"

"The juice is on me." Steve lifted his glass in a toast, grinning at the circle of faces. "Maybe today's the big day for all of us, and Chipper's the first at bat for the rally."

"I'll drink to that!" Matt lifted his glass, and everyone joined in.

Day Five and Counting

Sharron looked around the table, unsure how Steve's exuberance would be received. Tug Thompson's parents had been waiting longer than any of them for some glimmer of good news; six days now since the ATV accident took his leg and still no sign of consciousness. But at least he was stable. Wendy was still going downhill. Even so, as Sharron searched each face every one looked genuinely happy about her son's progress. Hope was definitely a welcome guest.

When Chipper came back from surgery, his parents were waiting at his station in ICU. Dr. Walker gave them the report.

"Everything has been cleaned out and closed up now, all wounds taken care of. There will be some scarring, but we are satisfied that things will heal nicely. We're also encouraged with his responsiveness. He's under some heavy medication for pain right now, but as he emerges from the sedation, I think we just might see some increased brain activity. Keep talking to him, and let me know what responses you can draw." He smiled his assurance and turned to go, then almost as an afterthought said, "By the way, I plan on removing the respirator tomorrow. I think Chipper is ready to start breathing on his own."

After two long hours of nothing but steady breathing, Chipper finally began to twitch and stir. Sharron took his hand and leaned in.

"Chipper? Chipper, it's Mum. Dad's here too. We want you to try to wake up now. If you can hear me, move your foot. Move your foot, Chipper."

Chipper

Chipper stirred again and Sharron felt his hand tighten slightly around her own. She smiled at Steve across the bed, then continued talking in her son's ear.

His responsiveness increased gradually as the afternoon wore on. At one point, he winced and grimaced, then began to thrash about in his bed. Steve anxiously buzzed the nurse. Chipper was twisting and writhing amid the tubes. Fearing he would pull out the IV needles, Steve held onto Chipper's arms.

"He might be hurting," the nurse ventured. She adjusted the medication in the IV and he soon began to calm down. He slept some, but was so restless that Steve and Sharron didn't dare leave his side for long.

It was early evening when Paula came for Chipper's sponge bath.

"I'm glad you're here." Sharron stood up, ready to help. "Chipper has had quite a day and so have I. I have so many questions, I made a list."

The two of them were talking and carefully sponging when Sharron lifted his hospital gown to start washing Chipper's stomach. He wrenched to one side and began thrashing violently. Sharron jumped back in shock. The nurse lunged forward and held his shoulders, talking to him calmly until he was still again.

"What brought that on?" Sharron asked. "More pain?"

Paula shook her head. "I don't know. But I think we'd best let him rest now." She pulled the curtains closed and turned off the lights. "I do know this. He's getting stronger."

When Steve came, he listened thoughtfully as she reported the incident. "I've never seen such a violent reaction from him. He must have had a real surge of pain that the monitors didn't pick up."

"I think it was the bath," Steve said.

"What?"

"The bath. You know how modest he is. I think Chipper's more conscious than we know. He reacted to something he didn't like. It seems to me," Steve took his wife's hand, smiling, "that our son is doing just what we want him to do. I think he's coming around."

Turning . . . turning
Spinning
Can't stop
Sticky black webs
Holding, jerking
Throbbing head
It hurts . . . it hurts!
Fading now
One . . . two . . . three . . .

What is it?
Wet, rubbing
No . . . stop!

9

"Doctor"

Early morning sunlight crept through the window with a warm honey glow that made the hospital lamp pale.

"How's he doing?" Steve asked.

Sharron blinked awake from a restless doze in the chair and tried to focus her eyes on her husband. She answered him with an automatic smile and a shrug of her shoulders.

"About the same."

"And you?" His eyes followed her as she moved to Chipper's bedside, hands braced on the rail. "Didn't sleep much, did you."

"This restlessness is tough to watch," she said. "I asked Dr. Walker about it last night and he said Chipper's really struggling inside right now. His mind is fighting to figure out what's happened. The agitation and thrashing are involuntary physical responses to his confusion."

Steve turned to face the window and let out a long, slow breath before speaking.

"Did the doctor give you any idea how long he'll be like this?"

"No, not really, but . . ." Sharron hesitated.

"What?"

"I've talked with families who have been here for months. We still have a long stretch ahead of us." Sharron waited for Steve to respond. When he didn't, she went to his side and slipped her arm through his.

"You're not losing hope now, are you Steve?"

He turned and took her hand. "Of course not. He's a Mangum, isn't he? He'll break all the records for getting better."

Sharron was watching her husband's face closely.

"What?"

"Something is bothering you, beneath all this talk of breaking records. What's on your mind?"

With a heavy sigh, he sank into the chair and looked up. "I just came from the financial office. Our bill for all of this is already over $100,000. There's no way in the world we can come up with that kind of money."

Sharron managed to hide her shock at the enormous sum. She knelt in front of him.

"We'll work it out. Remember what they told us when we first came here? There are ways . . . Medicaid, loans, grants. I know there will be programs we can qualify for." She lay her head on his lap and continued talking softly. "And things are going great at the shop. Doneva calls almost every day. She says business is rolling in. When I get back to work, and you're back on the job—"

"That's just it, Sharron," Steve interrupted. "We can't both just go back to work. Who knows how long Chipper will need constant care, even after he goes home. Don't you see? He's . . . it's not going to be like it was."

Sharron sat back at his somberness, but clung to her determination to comfort him. "Of course things will be different, at first. But eventually things will get back to normal, and then . . ." The look on Steve's face cut her off. There was a long span of silence, both thinking things neither dared say out loud. When Steve finally spoke, his voice was distant.

"I'm going to have to leave soon and go back to work."

Sharron stood and walked to the bedside, her back to Steve. "I can't be here without you."

Before Steve could respond, Tina came in, chattering her usual morning optimism.

"Well, looks like we survived another night. And what a beautiful summer morning it is, the kind that almost sings with the promise of good things, huh?" She began checking the monitors and jotting down information.

"I understand they'll be in to remove Chipper's respirator today. Soon we're going to see if this boy has anything he wants to say to us. What do you think about that, Mum?"

Sharron tried to sound excited. "It's great!"

Tina, too sharp to be fooled, gave her a questioning look before continuing.

"Listen, Mom and Dad, it takes most of the day to wean him off the machine. So I'll be right here if Chipper needs anything. Why don't you two take a little time off? Go get some breakfast, take a walk."

It took a little convincing, but Steve and Sharron decided to take Tina up on her offer. Maybe things wouldn't loom so grim after a shower and a little fresh air.

Throughout the day the respiratory therapist turned the oxygen to lower and lower levels, forcing Chipper to do more of his own breathing. Now it was time for the final step, and he carefully pulled the long hose from Chipper's throat and replaced it with a small oxygen tube in his nose. For the first time in six days, Chipper was breathing on his own.

It was the perfect day to receive the bouquet of balloons. A nurse brought them in, tied them to the foot of the bed, then handed the card to Steve.

"Who sent them?" Sharron asked, stretching to look over Steve's shoulder.

Steve handed her the card and turned away, hoping to hide his emotions.

Chipper

"Well, Chipper, look at this. Your swim team wants you to hurry back." Bending to kiss Chipper's cheek, she added, "You just wait until I tell Coach Coston that you held your breath for six days, then he'll really know he has a star on his team!"

The Therapist told them to wait a day before trying to get Chipper to talk. His throat was rubbed raw by the respirator and needed time to heal, and the added task of breathing was taking most of his energy. Steve and Sharron both sat with Chipper, doing all they could to calm him when he was awake. He slept a lot. Sharron took the time to catch up on her journal.

"The only way we can tell he's awake is that he tosses and turns like he's having a nightmare," she wrote. "It breaks my heart to see him so restless. I hope he moves past this stage quickly, for his sake and for mine.

"Finally tonight, we may have found a way to help him relax. We turned on his favorite movie, *The Little Mermaid*, and the moment the music started he calmed right down. Maybe tonight we can both get some much needed rest. Tomorrow is another big day. We'll find out if our son can still talk."

For the first time in a week Sharron slept all night in the parents' room. Steve came for her at daybreak. After organizing her few belongings in a corner, they listen with heartfelt concern as the Thompsons told of their own son's struggles. Tug had remained listless and unresponsive since his arrival at the hospital. His temperature was alarmingly high, and doctors weren't sure why, nor could they determine why nothing seemed to help. Steve and

Sharron offered what encouragement they could, then headed back to check on Chipper.

"Kinda makes you grateful for your own problems, huh?" Steve observed, stepping behind his wife to let a nurse-driven wheelchair pass.

"I guess," Sharron sighed. "The hardest thing for me right now is watching Chip acting so violent. It's not like him at all."

Even as they pushed through the double doors, they could see their son rolling and churning and flailing his arms.

"Now you rascal," Tina was saying. "You can't be pulling these tubes out like this."

They hurried to his bedside, and Steve put his face right next to his son's. Slowly, calmly, barely above a whisper, he talked until Chip quieted down again.

"That's got to make you feel good, Dad," Tina said as she dealt with the dislodged wires. "And your timing was perfect. A few more minutes of that break dancing would have caused us some major wiring problems." Tearing extra pieces of adhesive tape from a roll, she wrapped and stuck until Chipper's arms looked like a mummy's. She then wrapped soft white cords around his wrists and ankles and tied him to the bed. "Let's see you get out of that, Houdini. At least it should hold things together until this afternoon."

"This afternoon?" Sharron turned to ask. "What's happening this afternoon?"

"I know you aren't going to like this, but Dr. Walker wants him back in surgery. He wants to insert a line

directly into his heart to take the place of these IV's. Chipper won't be able to pull it out. It will make things a lot safer for him."

Sharron started to argue Chipper's case—two surgeries and one respirator removal in three days! But Tina countered with her usual reply: "Doctor's orders."

"Yes, I know," Sharron joined in on the next phrase. "And I don't argue with experience."

Tina flashed a smile at Steve. "She's learning."

"So when is this next 'little surgery'?"

"He's waiting until this afternoon so we can take a shot at getting Chipper to talk to us this morning. We have the best chance when he's rested." Tina bent over Chipper and looked at him earnestly. "You're just aching to come out, aren't you? I can feel it. We're going to use all the magic we know to help you unlock the doors." Straightening up again, she quietly stepped out of the room, leaving the Mangums to watch and wait.

Focused on a paperback in her lap, Sharron found herself inhaling and exhaling to the familiar rhythm of her son. Suddenly his breathing lightened a little, prompting Sharron to look up. She was amazed, almost startled when she saw that his eyes were open.

"Chipper!" she cried.

He blinked and focused briefly on her face. A flash of uncertainty and confusion passed through his eyes before his lids slowly half closed, twitched, and closed altogether.

"His eyes were open. He looked at me!" she said, first to herself, then loud enough to wake Steve. "Call Tina."

"Doctor"

Steve buzzed the nurse and moved his chair close to the head of the bed. Putting his mouth right next to Chipper's ear he began, unaware of a gathering audience.

"Hello Chipper. How are you feeling?"

Chipper lay motionless.

"Chipper, can you hear me? It's Dad. It's Dad, Chip. Listen to me, Son. The doctor says you need to try to talk. Mum and I are right here with you. We want you to talk to us. Try very hard, Chipper."

Chipper's eyelids fluttered briefly. Doctor Walker nodded for Steve to go on.

"That's it, Son, keep at it. You can do it. Please, talk to us."

Again a fluttering, and then the lids opened slightly. Sharron stood on the other side of the bed, waiting, listening, barely breathing.

"Yes. Yes. Come on, Chipper. Go ahead. Say it."

Chipper's mouth trembled, jerked, and opened slightly. Then, in a thin, raspy voice, he said,

"Doc-tor . . . "

Thick, black water
Sucking me down . . . down
Smothering . . . choking!
Gasping hot
Burning air
Breathe . . . breathe

Waves of music

Chipper

Swaying
Floating

"Chipper, talk . . . "

Talk . . . talk
Talk!
"Doc-tor . . . "

10
Rehab

The moment she clocked in for the night shift Paula hurried to Chipper's bedside.

"You got him to talk! I love starting my shift with such good news." She touched Chipper's cheek. "Nice work, Champ. Congratulations!"

Chipper

"It's been an up-and-down day, that's for sure," Steve told her. "One minute he's blinking and saying *doctor*, and the next he's twisting and thrashing like he's fighting a demon."

"You caught him at a rare moment," Sharron added. "He's finally sleeping. But when he's awake and one of those fits starts . . . I don't know, it's just not Chipper. Something must be bothering him."

Paula listened as they recounted events of the day, then tried to ease their worry.

"We expect some agitation. In fact, we're happy to see it. But too much can mean he's trying to tell us something. I'll keep a close watch on him tonight and see if I can tell what's going on." The nurse flashed a reassuring smile. "Now, why don't you two head to the parents' room and turn in for the night? You're going to burn yourselves out."

"No, I'm OK," Sharron spoke. "I can't rest at all when I'm away from him."

Paula turned to Steve. "Is there any hope of changing her mind?"

"If there is, I haven't discovered it in the twenty years I've known her." He bent down and gave his wife a quick kiss. "You really do need a break. I'll be back in a few hours to spell you off."

Sharron wrapped a gray flannel blanket around her shoulders and posted herself like a night guard a foot from Chipper's bed. Trying hard to relax and empty her mind, she watched his chest rise and fall in slow rhythm.

In ICU there was no such thing as bedtime. All night machines clicked and beeped, lights flashed, beds rolled in and out, nurses padded back and forth, their hushed voices distinct across stations. The constant activity kept Sharron half awake and conscious of her throbbing concern for her son. Nor could she forget the other small patients who filled the room. She'd seen more young lives end here than she cared to remember. The distress nagged worse than a headache, chasing away any hope of rest.

At 3:00 A.M. Chipper started churning again. Sharron took his hand, tried talking to him, rubbed his back, even began singing. But he just got worse. Tossing and writhing between the sheets, he started to cough, to choke.

Sharron jumped up frantically and tried to hold his jerking shoulders.

"You're OK, Chipper, you're OK. Doctor!"

She leaned over the bed, struggling at once to restrain him and to secure his attachments.

Paula was there, supporting his back as they tilted him upright. It took both of them to hold him until he quit gagging and gradually settled back.

"What was that all about?" Sharron asked, still trembling.

"I'm not sure," Paula told her. "I know he hates these tubes and needles, but I think it's more than that. It could be the constant lights and noise of this unit." She made a note on his chart, paused and watched him a moment. "Sometimes the mind gets stuck in time, stalled at the moment of the injury. The fear just won't go away."

Heartsick, Sharron sank back into her chair, "You mean he's still living that horrible moment when the tree hit! No wonder he—"

Chipper

Paula broke in.

"We'll pull him out of it, Mom. I'm recommending they move him to a private room, where the environment can be more controlled. Immediately."

By 5:00 A.M., Chipper had a new address: #2105 REHAB.

He arrived in his new room looking like he'd run a marathon. Sharron wiped the sweat from his face with a cool cloth, smoothed his bedding, then turned out the lights. For the next six hours he hardly stirred.

Steve and Sharron spent the morning sprucing up the room. They taped up pictures of family and friends, tied balloons to the bed, organized their personal things. Plants and flowers soon brightened the windowsill, cards decorated the counter. By lunchtime a cot and some extra bedding had been delivered, and the small room was as cheery and comfortable as they could make it.

"I don't know about Chipper, but I'm feeling better already," Sharron said, stretching to shove her emptied suitcase onto a closet shelf.

"It's starting to look downright homey in here," Steve agreed. "And from the way Chipper is sleeping, I think it's just what he needed."

It was just what they needed too. By midmorning Sharron was stretched out in slumber on the cot, Steve slumped asleep in a chair.

Look out! It's falling!
Thunder
Light flashing

Rehab

Cracking, crushing
Run!

"You're OK, Chipper, you're OK . . .
Doctor!"

No!
I can't . . . breathe . . .
Doctor . . . help me!

11

New Faces

"**W**ell now, which one of you is my patient?"

Sharron blushed. "Just follow the tubes, Dr. Walker." She rolled off Chipper's bed and walked stiffly to a chair. "Whenever I stopped rubbing his back, he twitched his shoulder and started stirring. So I kept rubbing."

"You mean you spent the entire night like that?"

"I'll do whatever it takes to keep him calm," she shrugged.

Steve sat up in the cot, rubbing his back. "I think she had the better spot."

The doctor chuckled. "Must have been quite a night."

"We all did fine," Sharron replied. "Chipper seemed much more relaxed. I hope it continues, I can't bear seeing him lose control like he was doing in ICU."

"Actually," Dr. Walker replied, "he's not losing control so much as struggling to regain control. His mind is working hard. There will likely be seizures—"

"Seizures!" Sharron gasped, terrified by the word alone. "Is that what's been happening to him?"

"It could be part of it," he explained. "And if he is having seizure activity, I'm afraid it's likely to continue."

"Oh dear," she sighed. "How long will we have that to worry about?"

"There are no absolutes with brain trauma patients, but he could experience them off and on for the rest of his life."

"The rest of his life?" This time it was Steve who voiced alarm. "But what about . . . sports? Camping? What about being a normal kid?"

"A normal kid?" the doctor smiled. "What's that?"

Voices sounded in the hallway and several doctors and nurses appeared. "Are you ready for us?" one of them asked.

"Come in," Dr. Walker motioned. "This is Dr. Tait. She and her staff will be coordinating Chipper's rehabilitation. From now on, she's in charge."

Steve rose to shake her hand. It wasn't often his six-foot frame stood eye-level to a woman.

"Good to meet you both." Her handshake was solid and her gray eyes penetrating. She turned back to her colleagues. "OK, boys, let's go for it."

Positioning the group in a half circle at the bedside, Dr. Tait motioned to Steve. "Mr. Mangum, if you'd like to stand right here, you can help us."

"Help you what?" Steve asked, puzzled.

"We're going to stand him up."

"What?" Sharron made no attempt to hide her shock. "How can someone who's not even conscious be expected to stand up?"

Dr. Tait gave her a patient smile. "How can he ever know we expect him to stand up if we don't give him the chance to try?"

Carefully, they slipped Chipper's legs off the edge of the bed.

"That's it. Now let's sit him up. Gradually now . . . good."

Chipper was standing—or at least stretched upright, with someone holding every limb and joint.

"How's that, Chipper? My goodness, look at you! Doesn't this feel great!" Dr. Tait showered praise. "Look at that. Did you see how he caught himself? He's actually trying to balance. That's wonderful, Chipper! Just right!"

On Dr. Tait's signal they carefully lowered him back and lifted his legs onto the bed. During the process, his eyes fluttered, half opened. Obviously delighted by his efforts, Dr. Tait turned to Sharron, who still stood gaping.

"He was ready for that," she assured. "He did great."

As the group filed from the room, Dr. Walker paused at the door. "I know we're pushing him, but there's a learning window that shuts tight if we don't catch it open. Dr. Tait knows what she's doing. You'll see."

Sharron sat back in her chair and closed her eyes.

"I think that was harder for you than it was for Chip," Steve observed. "I want you to try to rest awhile." He'd barely closed the door when a vigorous knock shook it.

"Hi. I'm Ramona, your personal laundress." A perky, white-aproned woman popped in. Her face was etched deep with lines left over from a thousand smiles. A spry bandanna kept her gray hair tightly tucked away.

"I'm on a quest," she bubbled. "I know I have the perfect quilt for this boy, and I aim to find it. Tell me about him. His favorite color, holiday, stuff like that. What does this rascal do for fun?"

Within the hour Ramona pushed back through the door, arms stacked with handmade quilts. Covering Chipper's bed with a bright red Scottish plaid, she teased, "Now, son, when you give a bagpipe concert, I plan to do the Highland Fling, and believe me, that'll be worth seeing!"

Stretching and puffing, she hung two lively sports quilts on the wall.

"And this one's for you, Mom." She wrapped a beautiful pink-and-white-heart-covered quilt around Sharron's shoulders. "Now, dear, is there anything else I can do?"

Sharron could not help laughing at this grandma's energy. "Do you do this for everyone?"

Her returning smile was wistful. "I do what I can."

Chipper

Once again, the door had just closed when another knock came, a light tap-tapping.

"I wonder if all newcomers get this kind of attention?" Sharron murmured, shuffling to the door. Opening it, she just stood and looked.

Steve called from behind her, "Can we help you?"

Struggling out of her stupor, Sharron stood back to let the stranger enter.

He was small framed, of medium height, and wore casual Levi's and a loose T-shirt. His thin face was covered with a wiry beard and mustache; his wavy, dark hair reached his shoulders. He smiled a thin smile, pulling off his wire-rimmed glasses.

"Actually, I'm here to help you. Or your son." His voice was quiet and matter-of-fact as he walked to the bedside. He drew a small glass container from his pocket and stooped to wave it under Chipper's nose. "I'm Mark Cantor."

"You're the speech therapist?" Sharron realized the doubt in her voice sounded rude. "I . . . we were told we might meet you today," she stammered, trying to sound less surprised than she felt. Steve stood to offer his hand.

"Steve Mangum. And my wife, Sharron."

Mark nodded and continued moving the bottle under Chipper's nose for several seconds. "Aha! Swallowing exercise successful." He grinned and kept talking as he shook Steve's hand. "If I can get that initial reaction when I put a strong odor under the patient's nose, I have a starting point. Did you see how his eyes and nose watered? Then I look for the swallowing response, and he did it beautifully.

He's ready for speech therapy. I suggest we bring him on down to the lab. Let's see, I could be ready for him by 4:00 this afternoon."

"What?" Sharron left her chair. "Do you realize this child was just brought here from Intensive Care so he could have some peace and quiet? You want him in speech therapy when he . . . he has hardly opened both eyes at once? This child is still in a coma!" Sharron took a deep breath and glared at the man who stood over her son. Mark Cantor screwed the lid back on the glass bottle, dropped it into his shirt pocket, folded his hands calmly behind his back and looked at Sharron.

"If moving Chipper to my lab is a problem for *him*," he subtly emphasized the last word, "we will make other arrangements. Nice meeting you."

Sharron stared after him, stood and followed to the doorway, then turned abruptly when he was gone.

"Can you believe that? I hope they don't expect me to turn my son over to some born-again hippie just because he sticks a bottle under Chipper's nose and says, 'he swallowed.' Who does he think he is?" She paced to the bedside, looked down at Chipper, then turned again to Steve. "Don't we have any say in what they do with our son? For $100,000.00, you'd think so!"

Chipper started to twitch in his bed, and Sharron lowered her tone. "He's just not ready for this."

Steve stood and walked to his wife's side. "No one said Chipper is going anywhere," he said quietly. "Maybe there are other . . . options." He took Sharron by the hand and they headed for the nurses' station.

Chipper

"That man who just left our room. Mark Cantor. What do you know about him?"

The nurse looked up from her computer.

"Mark? Oh, he's a wonderful man. A miracle worker, some say. We have several speech therapists here and they're all good, but Mark's the best. You're lucky to have him. In fact, when he read through Chipper's file, he was so intrigued by it he requested your case."

"But is he really qualified?" Sharron stuttered.

"Qualified?" the nurse laughed. "He's a leading authority on communicative and cognitive disorders. Flies all over the country giving lectures. Frankly I was surprised he asked to add Chipper to his hectic schedule." She rose and began filing a handful of papers. "If there is anyone who can teach your son to talk again, it's Mark Cantor!" She paused. "Why do you ask? Is there a problem?"

Steve and Sharron exchanged glances that were quickly made to look innocent.

"No, no. No problem."

Arms holding
Pulling
Hands squeezing
Lifting
Head pounding
Spinning
Faces, faces
Who are you?

New Faces

"OK, down . . . easy . . .
There!"

What is it?
Don't like it
It stinks!

12

I Am

At 4:00 P.M. Chipper was sitting in Mark Cantor's speech therapy room, strapped in a wheelchair, with all his attendant machinery still attached. Sharron and Steve were seated beside him, catching their breath. The move from Chipper's room had taken them a full thirty minutes.

I Am

"I just can't believe they are putting him through this so soon!" Sharron said. When Steve did not respond, she sat back with a sigh. "I guess I'm mother henning again, huh?"

Steve gave his wife a quick smile, then turned to focus on Chipper. The truth was, he too felt things were moving a bit fast.

Chipper hung limp, strapped in his chair, head wobbling, eyes half-closed. Reaching out, Steve removed the blanket covering his son's legs, readjusted his gown, and gave him a pat on the knee.

"Let's give it our best shot, OK, Champ?"

It was a room made for children. A child-sized table sat by the window, surrounded with small chairs. A low shelf housed toys, stuffed animals, and a crate of simple everyday objects: shoes, dishes, balls, books. Warm sunlight beamed through a large window, spilling over Chipper and onto the floor.

As Chipper's monitors clicked their steady rhythms in the still room, Sharron studied the artwork that decorated the walls: smiling stick figures holding hands, crooked yellow suns, dancing blue dinosaurs. Who were the children behind these scribbled masterpieces pinned proudly to the wall? What had brought them here? Where were they now?

Mark Cantor entered and politely instructed Steve and Sharron to move back and participate only if invited. His entire focus then fell upon Chipper.

"Chipper. Hello." He spoke slowly, gently, as if speaking to a frightened two-year-old. He pointed to himself: "I am Mark. Mark—" smiling, waiting, his gaze intent. He touched Chipper's arm. "Chipper." He repeated the name

several times. Then reaching behind himself he pulled a bright red ball from the crate, never taking his eyes off Chipper's face. "Ball." Again he repeated the word. Chipper sat motionless, his expression a sleepy stare.

Sharron shifted in her seat, trying to block out a picture of herself talking like that to Chipper when he was a grown man. She suddenly wanted to leave, go back to the room and have a good cry.

The session dragged on, Mr. Cantor waiting long between each word. Steve found himself searching the room for a clock. Surely they had been there long past an hour, and he had yet to see a clue that Chipper even knew he was being talked to.

"Do you want to talk, Chipper?" the therapist was saying. "I know you hear me." He knelt down in front of the wheelchair and took Chipper's limp hand. His voice stayed patient and clear. "What would you like to say?"

Chipper tried to raise his head. He opened his eyes. Mark Cantor sank a little lower, moving his face into Chipper's view.

"You want to talk, don't you, Chipper?"

"Doc . . . tor," Chipper stammered.

"That's it! Good!"

There was a stretch of silence.

"Chipper," Mark sat forward, his face close to Chipper's. "Do you like to sing?"

"Doctor," Chipper said again, but this time the word sounded different, not so mechanical.

"Chipper, will you sing for me?"

I Am

Chipper opened his mouth, but nothing came out. Tenderly, cautiously, Mark put his hand over Chipper's. "Sing," he whispered.

The room was still, hushed. Steve leaned forward, holding his breath. Chipper's eyes opened wide and focused on Mark Cantor's pleading face. Faintly, unsteadily, he began to sing.

"I am . . . a child . . . of God . . . and He has sent me here . . ."

For the first time during the session, Mark Cantor looked across the room at Steve and Sharron, his face a display of delight. Chipper kept singing, and the therapist signaled for them to join him.

"Lead me, guide me, walk beside me, help me find the way . . ."

Tears filled their eyes as they sang the chorus of Chipper's favorite childhood lullaby.

In the moment of awe that followed, Mark sat back and smiled. He touched Chipper's hand.

"That was beautiful, Chipper Mangum. Thank you."

Who are you?
Leave me alone.

"I know you hear me."

Go away
Can't talk . . . can't do anything

Chipper

"You want to talk, don't you, Chipper?"

Want to talk . . . want to . . .
"*Doc . . .tor.*"

"Good!"

Good . . . good

"Chipper, will you sing for me?"

Good . . . good . . . God
"*I am . . . a child . . . of God . . . *"
Yes . . . I am

"That was beautiful, Chipper Mangum! Thank you."

I am . . .
Chipper Mangum!
Thank you.

13

One Word at a Time

"Chipper, Baby. Come away from the door."

"Go!"

The eight-month-old fist pounded the screen door, popping it open. Dad took a flying leap for the porch step just as the plump legs were about to attempt the concrete stairway.

Chipper

"Did you hear that, Mum? He said *go!* But you can't go with Daddy, buddy. You better slow down, or you'll end up in a hospital. Don't you know these stairs are dangerous for a little Chipper-nipper like you?"

"Chipper, how did you get out of your crib? I swear, you're going to wear Mum out, trying to keep up with you. He said what?"

"*Go.* Didn't you hear him? His first word. Better write that down, Mum."

"Why does that not surprise me? Go, go, go. That's my Chipper-boy."

"Come on, Chipper, now say, *Daddy.* Say, *go Daddy,* and I'll take you anywhere."

"One word at a time, Daddy. This kid's not even nine months, and you got him walking down stairs and making speeches. Holy Toledo."

"Didn't I tell you he'd break every record? And the stair walking was his own idea. We've got to fix that screen door. Takes more than a latch to hold a Mangum man in, huh Champ? Here, Mum, better not let this guy out of your sight. Daddy's got to get to work."

"Come here, you. Don't you think I have anything better to do than keep my eyes on you? Well you're right. Looks like Mum's gonna have to stick by you like old jam on a doorknob."

"Steve—do you remember his first word?" Sharron spoke from the bedside where she had been staring down at Chipper's sleeping face.

"Sure do." Steve looked up from his newspaper. "I'm the one he said it to, remember? He said *go*. And he's been a goer ever since, hasn't he?"

The light tapping on the door signaled Mark Cantor's entrance. He finished a conversation with a passing orderly in the hall and stepped just inside the doorway.

"About yesterday's experience," he began, giving his glasses a habitual push. "When your son began to sing, it was . . . most unusual. In the fourteen years I've been working with brain trauma kids, well, that was as close to a miracle as anything I've experienced." He cleared his throat. "But I don't want to create unrealistic expectations. We've got a tough road ahead."

"It was a miracle," Sharron heard herself tell him.

Raising dark heavy brows, he nodded. "Miracles come as a result of good hard work, Mrs. Mangum. Both of you had a part in what happened." He turned to leave. "By the way, I want to meet with Chipper alone in his session this morning."

Sharron's smile instantly dropped. She turned to Steve, her mouth open to protest, but he held up his hand.

"He knows what he's doing, Sharron. After yesterday he could ask for a session at the top of Mount Timpanogos and I'd go for it."

Preparing Chipper for his 10:00 A.M. speech therapy session occupied the entire morning. Sharron watched Warren, the orderly, wheel away her son, droopy and lethargic. She fought the anxiety creeping up inside her. She was grateful when the door swung open and Terie and Scott walked in.

Chipper

"You should see all the stuff people sent from home," Terie bubbled. But her face fell when she saw the empty bed. "Where's Chip?"

"Speech therapy," her dad explained. "Let's see all this stuff."

Soon the small counter was covered with videos, pictures, cards, letters, posters.

"Look at this; Arron sent him his Bruce Hurst! Chip'll love adding that to his card collection." Scott pulled two more treasures from his overnight bag, an autographed baseball from Chipper's Little League team and a Sony Walkman.

"You're going to leave this?" his dad questioned, helping him with the stereo. It was Scotty's prized possession.

"You know how much Chipper gets into music. Maybe it will help."

Terie was more interested in where Chipper was. "He's in speech therapy again, huh? I can't believe he's getting better so fast. When can he come home?"

Sharron had called home the night before to tell the family how Chipper sang in Mr. Cantor's office. They were so excited she didn't add that he hadn't spoken a word since then. She realized now she must have been overenthusiastic in her report, but didn't want to put a damper on their hope.

"He's doing better, but we still don't know a lot about the future."

Chipper looked entirely spent when Warren finally wheeled him through the door. His eyes were barely open and his head hung, lolling to one side.

One Word at a Time

"Hey, Bro, the haircut looks awesome!" Scotty's enthusiasm sounded forced, and he tried to do better. "I brought you some neat stuff, Chip . . ." his voice faded off in uncertainty as Chipper stared blankly at the floor.

"You're Chipper's brother?" Warren tried to ease the awkwardness. "How about giving me a hand here."

Scott helped Warren lift Chipper onto the bed and adjust his monitor wires.

"He still doesn't know who we are, does he?" Terie whispered to her mother, disappointment clear in her voice.

"I know it's hard, Honey. Dad and I aren't even sure he recognizes us. He's exhausted right now. With some rest and time, he'll start recognizing things, I'm sure."

"Wait—" Terie was digging in her purse. Grinning, she produced a picture of Buddy, Chipper's dog. She hurried to his bedside. "Look, Chipper. I have a picture of Buddy. You remember Buddy, don't you, Chip?"

Chipper opened his eyes wide and struggled to sit up. Terie was beaming. "I knew he would know Buddy. You couldn't forget Buddy, could you?"

Chipper's bottom lip began to tremble, and he tried to reach out to take the picture, but his hand fell limp in front of him. He began sobbing, and then started thrashing about violently in his bed. Terie jumped back in alarm.

"I'm sorry, I didn't think . . ." she mumbled through tears as Warren and Steve fought to hold Chipper down and calm him. "I thought the picture would make him happy—"

"It's OK, Terie," her mother reassured. "Your brother is full of surprises right now."

Chipper

When Warren pulled a sticker from his pocket and put it on Chipper's finger, he immediately stopped thrashing and held up his hand, smiling like a two-year-old with a special prize. He settled back in his bed and let Sharron rub his back until he fell asleep.

Mr. Cantor stopped by to report on the morning therapy session. The family was hoping he could shed some light on Chipper's latest upheaval.

"No one can say exactly what Chipper is thinking and feeling right now," Mr. Cantor said, his arms crossing his clipboard as he leaned against the doorframe.

"But I can tell you what he needs: patience, peace and quiet, and a lot of time." He looked around the room at the troubled faces. "It's as if his brain has been scrambled. His mind is like a huge filing cabinet, and all of its contents have been not only spilled but cut into tiny pieces and scattered by the wind. Chipper is trying desperately to put all the pieces together and refile the information. Some of the pieces are gone. His brain has to build new information pathways. He must relearn all that was lost and at the same time refile what is there but jumbled. This is no easy task. Not many kids are able to accomplish it."

Steve jumped in: "Wait a minute. Are you saying you don't think Chipper will be able to pull this off? That yesterday's experience in your office was . . . some sort of fluke?"

"No, Mr. Mangum, I'm not saying that at all. Like I told you earlier, it was as close to a miracle as anything I've seen. And I'm confident that Chipper will continue to progress. But you must understand the difficulty of the task your son is up against. You must work with me to make his world simple for awhile."

"I'm confused," Sharron admitted. "We've been told to talk with him continually, to seek every opportunity to stimulate his mind so that no learning opportunities are missed. Now you say we are not to stimulate him too much?"

"I wish the procedures were clearer, Mrs. Mangum. But the truth is we must do both. Talk to him, but not tire him. Stimulate him, but not beyond his limits."

"And how are we to know his limits?"

The therapist sighed. "That's the tricky part. Perhaps I can help." He sat down and wrote a list of suggestions and rules for Chipper's activities and taped it to the door.

Sharron looked it over. "I guess we just take it one day at a time, huh?"

"No. One word at a time."

14
Spirit

Chipper slept fifteen hours. Terie and Scotty hoped he would wake before they needed to leave, but finally had to be content with the thought that they would see him awake next trip.

"By then, you might even be able to talk with him," their mother smiled through the car window. She and Steve waved them off into the traffic, Steve calling his usual, "Drive carefully!"

Sharron started back to Chipper's room, the need to be by his side always pulling at her. Steve stood motionless on the sidewalk, his eyes still on the road.

"Are you coming?" she asked.

"I probably should have gone home with them."

She stood several feet away, her expression saying, "We've been through this."

"The next chance I have, Sharron, I need to go home and back to work."

Her mouth was open to answer, but a sigh was all that came.

"I'll come back between runs," he continued. "I won't stay away long. You understand why I can't just hope someone else takes care of the financial end of this, don't you? I need to do what I can." He paused. She remained silent. "Sharron, I can't expect them to hold my job for me forever." Again he looked for her response.

She laced her arm through his and started walking down the shrub-lined path back to the hospital. They pushed through the turning doors and stood in front of the lobby elevator. She wanted to tell him she understood, but fear of being without him made the words catch in her throat.

"If I get another chance to ride home with someone, I think I—we need to seriously consider it." His voice faded into the sound of the elevator door opening.

Chipper

The chance came sooner than either of them expected. Doneva Hunt stopped in with a box of hot pink baseball caps she had made at the sewing shop. Embroidered across the front in bold white were the words, *You Should See The Tree!*

"Here you go, Chip." Doneva carefully placed a cap on Chipper's shaved head. "You'll be the first on the block to have one!"

By afternoon, the halls were filled with men, women, and kids dressed in white jackets, green scrubs, hospital gowns, and hot pink baseball caps. Mark Cantor came by wearing his and pulled Steve aside. They spoke together for a few minutes, shook hands, and parted company, grinning.

"What was that about?" Sharron questioned.

"Secrets," Steve teased. "I'll tell you when I get back this weekend."

"As if it won't be hard enough for me to wait. Come on, let me in on it," she pleaded.

Steve just smiled and led her down the hall to say good-bye to the Thompsons.

Tug was finally making some progress. His eyes were open, though in a blank stare, and he was sitting up. They fitted him with a hat, visited with the family for awhile, then moved on.

Being back in ICU stirred up uneasy memories, and Sharron searched for words of comfort to offer the Woods. Wendy was still in critical condition. Wishing they could do more, they offered a listening ear until it was time for

Spirit

Steve to go. Steve handed them several *You Should See The Tree* hats and bid them goodbye until the weekend.

Chipper was awake when they got back. Steve sat on his bed and tried to explain why he had to go. To his surprise, Chipper lifted his arms and wrapped them around his dad, crying and clinging to his neck. He did not loosen his grip until a nurse put a sedative in his IV. Only then did he relax and settle back into a deep sleep.

"I think you'd better give me a dose of that," Sharron told the nurse, attempting a smile. Steve held her, and this time it was Mum who clung to Dad's neck.

In the half-light of the new day Sharron quietly turned the pages of her journal. Words and names jumped out at her, replaying in her memory a scene here, a feeling there, as if her mind and heart were being run by a remote control scanning the channels. Finally coming to a blank page, she breathed deeply and began writing:

"Sunday, June 17. Father's Day. Day 12. My first day alone with my son. I'm scared!"

Staring at the page, she could write no more. Usually the journal was great therapy. Not this morning. Sharron closed the book and slipped out of the room. When she saw Debbie, she quickly dabbed her eyes. Debbie had faced countless surgeries with Bryn, yet remained so optimistic.

"Sharron. I understand Steve left yesterday. Are you doing all right?"

What was it about Debbie that made Sharron's true feelings surface like a cork in a sink?

"I can't do this alone, Debbie. I'm not as tough as you." She let the tears come.

Debbie took her arm. "I've thought the same thing about you. I guess no one's as tough as the person they're watching." They stood a moment. "Sharron, why don't you and Chipper come to church with little Bryn and me?"

Sharron fumbled for an excuse, but Debbie persisted. "I think it would be good for both you and Chipper. We love the meeting. It starts at 10:00. We'll stop by on our way."

So Sharron headed back to the room to begin the arduous task of getting Chipper ready for church. Without Steve's help, the job was exhausting. By the time she had Chipper dressed in sweat pants and a green scrub gown, she seriously doubted whether any meeting could be worth the effort.

"I thought this boy was hard to dress at age two," she sighed when Debbie wheeled Bryn through the doorway. "Guess I should quit complaining about how much weight he's lost, huh?" Listening to the chirpy sound of her own voice, Sharron wondered if she would spend the rest of her life pretending to be cheerful.

Debbie only smiled. She stepped over and helped Sharron strap Chipper in. The two wheelchairs rolled down the hallway like twin strollers.

As they neared the hospital chapel the way got crowded with churchgoers: children in wheelchairs, children laboring with silver-poled walkers, children slumped in their fathers' arms, children walking weakly between parents. Sharron was so absorbed in maneuvering her own load that she didn't take particular notice of the others until a wobbling boy in a rolling walker-rig blocked her way and she was forced to a standstill. She watched the parade of struggling kids. A bright-eyed toddler peered at her over his father's shoulder, his hairless head shiny, his thin arms coiled securely around his dad's neck.

"Hi!" he grinned down at her.

"Hello there, young man," she returned, immediately taken with his eyes and their dancing flecks of light. Body frail and clinging, eyes alive with life, he disappeared around the corner, replaced with an older girl and her mother, walking arm in arm, step in step. The girl struggled to force one rubbery leg in front of the other, tilting her head upward to beam at her mom every three or four steps. Smiling as she passed, Sharron steered around the twosome. Her feelings of aloneness were being swallowed up in this crowd of strangers, who did not feel like strangers at all. Stepping up her pace, she wheeled forward to catch up with Debbie and Bryn just as they were entering the chapel.

A tall man in a gray suit and red tie met them at the door.

"Hello there, Son. I'm Brother McKay. You look like a twelve-year-old, or I'd miss my guess. If you're a deacon, we could sure use your help with the sacrament."

Chipper had one eye partly open, but made no response. Sharron spoke up.

"This is Chipper. He is a deacon, but I'm afraid he won't be much help with the sacrament. His accident has severely limited—"

Brother McKay's hand on Sharron's shoulder stopped her. His direct gaze was also kind.

Chipper

"Accidents can do hard things to the body. But here, we focus on the spirit. Please, follow me."

Sharron held that thought and pushed along behind Brother McKay as he cleared the way to the line of deacons. He turned to position Chipper's wheelchair along the wall with several others, then escorted Sharron to a seat.

"We'll support his arms and guide him along. He'll be fine."

His confident but gentle manner helped loosen the tightening threads of uncertainty she felt. Still, she slid to the end of the bench where she could watch Chipper and get to him quickly if needed.

Waiting for the meeting to begin, she pondered Brother McKay's words: "We focus on the spirit." The thought brought to light in her mind a warming reality: her son's body may have been damaged, but his spirit was still strong, unharmed. His spirit was Chipper, right down to the core. She closed her eyes and whispered, "From now on, my Chipper, I will see your spirit first and your body second, in the true order of importance."

She relaxed and watched with a new sense of peace as the helpers guided Chipper along the rows, supporting his arms, steering his hands, gripping with him the silver tray of broken bread.

15

Colossus

The pattering rhythm of summer rain pulled Sharron's attention from her journal to the window. She watched the blurring polka dots merge and streak down the glass.

"It's the season of surprise," she finally wrote, "the time when Utah weather seems to take its cues from a rollercoaster, up and down, one day hot, the next drippy. I love it. But then, I've always liked rollercoaster rides."

She sat, smiling to herself, and was for a moment a young girl again, standing anxiously beneath the huge flashing sign: "COLOSSUS." Her memory brought back the clanking and churning of the bright red-and-yellow cars, the iron bar that clicked to her lap but felt much too loose to hold her in when the lurching and jerking began, clackety clack, clackety clack. Every squeak, groan, and pop of the cable said this time the old tracks and wires would not hold. Then came the teetering pause at the top of the wooden hill. Her wild screams sliced the air as the train began its downward plummet. The wind sucked each breath and the narrow track yanked at the rickety car until she felt sure she'd never survive.

But she always had, and would now, through all these ups and downs. She would climb off this emotional roller-coaster, the twists and jolts becoming a memory. Already she was getting better at recalling the scenes without reliv-ing the pain. Still, as she thought of the past week, it felt like the old Colossus.

"Hello there!"

Sharron was about to return the happy greeting when she realized the new nurse was talking to Chipper, who was awake and staring ahead. The grandmotherly woman sat on the side of the bed and took Chipper's hand. "My, my. They've got you attached to every contraption in this hospital. Well, my boy, we're going to wean you from them one at a time. And I think you and I will grow to be very good friends in the process."

As she beamed down at him, Chipper suddenly lurched forward, threw his arms around her neck, and cried out "Yes!" She laughed with delight and gave him a good hug back. Over Chipper's shoulder, her eyes met Sharron's.

"Hello! You must be his mother."

"And you must be a wizard!" Sharron exclaimed. "Do you know that *doctor* is the only word this child has spoken since we arrived two weeks ago? And the only other person he has hugged is his dad! But you . . . you, how did you do that?"

"Don't ask me. He gave me the hug."

Sharron sat dumbfounded. "Well, if my son is this excited about you, I'd better know your name."

"BarDonna," the nurse smiled.

"BarDonna, I'm impressed."

"Well I have to confess, I have a special attachment to brain-trauma kids. And when I heard Chipper's story, I knew this guy would be one of my prized patients. You see, my dear husband had an accident much like Chipper's, except his experience ended on the mountain, under the tree that was supposed to fall the other way."

"Oh. I'm so sorry."

"Well, it happened many years ago. But it kinda steered me to where I am now—helping these precious children, and loving every minute of it." Her focus returned to Chipper. "Dear me, he's nearly strangled by these tubes and machines," she sighed. "I know he needs 'em right now, but I wish I could make him more comfortable."

Chipper

Chipper seemed to understand what she was saying, and with a flip of his arm, he reached up and jerked the feeding tube from his nose.

"Oh, my! We can't be doing that, Child," she clucked. "I know it feels just awful, but Dr. Tait told me you have to keep it in until you start eating better on your own. When you do that, Chipper Boy, BarDonna will jerk that thing out for you! Well, speak of the devil."

"I hope I'm not thought of in that way," Dr. Tait chuckled as she walked to the bedside and helped reinsert the tube.

"I was just telling Chipper that he could take this thing out for good as soon as he started eating solids," BarDonna told her.

"That's right, Chipper," Dr. Tait leaned over him. "I want you to eat more." But Chipper had lapsed back into his staring-ahead mode. The doctor turned to Sharron. "I think he'll eat, with the right coaxing."

"It appears to me we have just the person to do that," Sharron smiled at BarDonna, who was busying herself tucking covers around Chipper's legs and fluffing his pillows.

After the doctor left, BarDonna waved down a candy striper and asked her to bring some tapioca pudding. Within the hour, she had Chipper eating.

"You are a wizard," Sharron said. "He doesn't even like that stuff!"

On Wednesday Chipper achieved a major conquest. The physical therapist was helping him through his usual routine. Assistants stood close, supporting his weight, helping him catch his balance as he grasped the bars along the walking pad. Chipper had been standing on his own unsteadily for a couple of days, but had made no attempt to take any steps—until that moment.

Trembling, he inched his left foot forward, then strained to pull the right one up. Cheers from the therapists brought a radiant grin, prompting another arduous effort.

"Way to go, Chipper! You did it. You're walking!"

Once he got the general idea, Chipper wouldn't give up until he had worked himself up to three all-by-himself steps.

That afternoon Wendy's brother and sister popped in. Twelve-year-olds Jesse and Josie were on their way to the Children's Recreation Room to make cookies, and wanted to take Chipper along. Sharron looked up to say no, but something . . . the eager expressions on the twins' faces? The memory of the positive experience of that morning? Something made her say, "Go for it, Chip!"

As the three of them wheeled out the door, Sharron had serious second thoughts. Summoning all her will power, she made herself stay in her seat.

"Fifteen minutes," she told herself. "I'll give them fifteen minutes before I go check on them. Nothing can happen in fifteen minutes . . ."

Fifteen long, watching-the-clock, pacing-the-floor minutes. Then she hurried to the Rec. Room. Taking a deep breath to attempt a casual entrance, she pushed open the doors.

Chipper

The picture she saw was worth framing. There was Chipper, standing at the counter. Jesse and Josie were on either side of him, and he was rolling cookie dough balls as though it were something he had been doing for ages. The twins were chatting and laughing, genuinely enjoying his crooked smiles and raspy laughter.

"Well, what do you know," Sharron said to herself. "I guess a lot can happen in fifteen minutes."

Thursday had been a rough day. Sharron let Chipper try to dress himself as Dr. Tait had recommended. But zippers, buttons, laces, even pants legs and shirt sleeves were too complicated. With every failed effort, Chipper grew more frustrated and angry.

"You can't take this personally, Sharron," Dr. Tait had reminded her. "We have to learn how fast to push him, and Chipper needs to learn it's not the end of the world if he can't put his pants on yet."

Chipper was already upset when she wheeled him into Mark Cantor's therapy room, and Sharron felt the full weight of the uphill ride before them.

Mr. Cantor began showing Chipper simple pictures. He recognized nothing, not even a cow or horse. The therapist attempted a series of eye and hearing tests, but even the simple yes-and-no questions proved more than Chipper could handle. His frustration grew. Finally, Mr. Cantor closed the book and leaned back.

"We're not getting anywhere with this series. I'll try it again in a few days."

Chipper suddenly stiffened and started pounding the arms of his chair and kicking his feet. The more they tried to soothe him, the harder he kicked and pounded. He thrust an arm out and struck his mother right in the face.

"Chipper!"

Mark Cantor stood. "We've pushed too far. Let's call it a day."

As they were leaving, Mr. Cantor pulled Sharron aside.

"It might be best if Chipper came alone a few sessions," he suggested. "You could use a rest from all this, Sharron. And I want to see how Chipper reacts without . . . extra influences in the room."

Sharron's chest was tight as she wheeled Chipper back. "Is that all I am?" she muttered to herself, "an extra influence?"

By evening she was weary and discouraged. She went through the routine of readying Chipper for the night, then sat down next to him on his bed.

"Oh, Son," she moaned. "I know how scared and frustrated you are. I'm frightened, too. I'm afraid you don't know your mum anymore, that you don't know how much I love you. It scares me that I can't help or comfort my own boy. I just wish I knew what you were thinking, feeling. Then maybe I would know what to do for you." She rested her head on his lap, staring at the floor. "Maybe . . . maybe I should go home for a while."

Chipper made a gasping sound that jerked Sharron's eyes to his face. He was looking at her through tear-filled eyes.

"No!" he cried. The word was firm and clear. Sharron threw her arms around him and held him close.

"Oh, Chipper. You do need me here, don't you."

Chipper

When Chipper finally loosened his grip, Sharron drew back and wiped away his tears. "Don't worry, I'll stay. We'll ride this out together, you and I."

16

Bubbles

A bubble blizzard swirled through the Rehab floor, one room at a time.

"I think we've created a bubble monster," Sharron laughed as she wheeled Chipper into Wendy's room for one more visit.

Chipper

Words or no words, Chipper left no doubt that today he wanted one thing only: to blow bubbles for every child on the Rehab floor.

It all started when BarDonna sat down with Chipper and taught him to blow bubbles. It took all morning, but Chipper finally caught on and maneuvered the wand from the bubble jar to his mouth–most of the time. Grinning with delight, he watched the bubbles drift and dance to the floor or pop like magic in the air in front of him. That's when BarDonna came up with the plan.

"You know, Chipper, there are a lot of children here who can't leave their beds. They'd love to see these bubbles! How about a bubble parade?"

Sharron had pushed him into a room where Brittany, an eighteen-month-old girl, sat crying in her bed. Chipper's bubbles were magical; they instantly caught her attention and the sobbing stopped. Seeing the child's tears replaced so quickly with laughter was all it took: Chipper was hooked.

Bubbles turned out to be the motivation to get Chipper to eat. "You can have the bubbles after you've eaten," Sharron would tell him. When a bowl of Apple Jacks was placed before him Friday morning, Chipper ate every bite, his eyes focused on the bubble jar across the room. Before his appointment with Mark Cantor, he had visited Brittany, Greg, Kory, Bryn, and Tug. Even the speech therapy room was filled with bubbles, and Sharron left therapist and patient playing *count and pop* as she headed for the nurses station to take a phone call.

Bubbles

"I'm on my way up," Steve's voice came over the line. "I'll be there in five hours. Tell Chipper not to put on any spectacular performances until I get there."

"Well if he does, I'll likely miss them too," Sharron told him. "He's scheduled for most of the day in therapy. I've been letting him go it alone. He seems to do better sometimes without Mother-Hen-Mum."

"I hope you're not taking it personally, Honey. Oh, by the way," Steve's voice turned playful, making her all the more anxious to see him. "I'm bringing a little surprise with me. Mr. Cantor and I have a new therapy cooked up for Chipper. See you in awhile."

"Steve! Tell me," Sharron called over the phone. "As if it's not hard enough for me to wait as it is." Too excited to resist, Steve shared the secret with his wife, but made her promise, "not a word to Chipper."

Sharron peeked in on the physical therapy session, wanting to cheer Chipper on, yet not anxious to see his face-first falls every time he forgot to move his right leg. Knowing the danger of even a minor bump to the head, the therapists never let Chipper hit the ground, but still, it was all too frightening for Sharron.

They worked for almost an hour before the therapists could convince Chipper to take a break. When they pulled out a Nerf ball, Sharron couldn't watch any longer. Just that morning, Ash had called with the news that Chipper had been picked for the Cedar National All Star team: honorary catcher. His dream had come true. Now she was watching her star catcher struggle just to stop a twelve-inch foam ball, let alone catch it.

Chipper

When therapy was over Sharron was hoping Chipper would forget about bubbles, he looked so exhausted. Not a chance. She hurried him through the rounds, hoping to get him back to the room in time to rest before his dad arrived. Finally making it to the last stop, Wendy's room, Sharron sank into a chair to visit with Matt and Marilyn while Chipper puffed at his wand. Jessie and Josie giggled and batted at the flurry of bubbles, competing to burst each one before it hit the floor. Wendy, to everyone's sorrow, sat out the bubble storm in a half-lidded gaze.

"They've upgraded her from coma to semi-coma, so I suppose they can see some change," Marilyn explained quietly. "Mark Cantor comes in every day to talk to her, but we don't know if anything is getting through. We pray for some sign, some response . . . I guess we just keep hoping."

Chipper suddenly stopped blowing and handed the bubble jar to his mom. He wheeled to Wendy's side and took her hand. Matt reached out and put his hand on both of them, smiling at Chipper.

"You know what she's going through, don't you, Pal?"

Sharron was quiet as she wheeled her son back down the hallway. Like the colors mixing and pulling in Chipper's bubbles, a spectrum of emotions churned inside her. Faces flashed in doorways, room after room, child after child. One room housed a nine-month-old victim of child abuse. In another rested a three-year-old who had been revived from drowning. They passed the room of a boy with a brain tumor, then that of a teen recovering from a self-inflicted gunshot wound to the head. There were victims of car and ATV accidents. Two rooms held children recovering from operations repairing birth defects.

"They're as fragile as your bubbles, Chipper," Sharron sighed. "I wish I could reach out and catch every one of them, not let any . . . hit the ground." She could have sworn she saw Chipper nod his head.

17

Buddy

It's about time!" Sharron jumped to her feet. "What did you do, stop for a game of golf?"

"What do you mean? I nearly broke the land speed record getting here!" Steve's cheerful tones always brought rays of light, and Sharron happily soaked them in. Pulling

Buddy

him into the room, she gave him a big hug before rousing Chipper.

"Hey, Champ," Steve bent and gently shook his son. "Wake up. I brought you a surprise."

Opening his eyes, Chipper let out a gasping "yes!" and grabbed his Dad in a sudden headlock.

"Yup! He's definitely improving," Steve worked an exaggerated gag in his voice. He winked at Sharron, obviously delighted with the greeting. "Come on, Son. Let's go for a little ride. There's something waiting for you outside."

Steve covered Chip's bald head with an All Stars cap, lifted him to his chair and wheeled him past the main floor and out to the hospital lawn. Chipper was caught up in the excitement and his arms and legs jerked and twitched as he looked around. His lopsided grin even spread a little to the right. As Steve pushed Chipper toward the evening shade of a big cottonwood, a furry face poked around the trunk and into view. With a throaty squeal, Chipper lurched out of his chair. Barely catching him, Steve helped seat his son safely on the grass. In one flying leap the splotchy brown weenie dog landed in the middle of Chipper's lap, smothering him with slobbery, long-tongued kisses. Tears of joy spilled down Chipper's cheeks, and Buddy licked at them, his tail beating time like a high-speed metronome. Steve and Sharron stood back, arm in arm, so thrilled with the scene all they could do was laugh.

The family played under the tree for close to an hour, until the sun dipped low and the air turned chill. "We've got to take him in," Sharron whispered, her motherliness taking over. Chipper threw his arms around his dog in one of his gridlock holds and looked up. It was clear he intended to go nowhere.

"He'll be right here waiting for you in the morning, Son," Steve promised. But Chipper held tight.

Sharron tried her luck. "You need to rest now, Chip, and so does Buddy."

But Chipper buried his face in the fur and clung.

"Wait!" Steve's eyes had their bright-idea twinkle, and Sharron watched with amusement as he picked Chipper up, dog and all, put them in the wheelchair and covered them both with the blanket. He wheeled the load in the door and past the nurses station, nodding a polite hello. Sharron followed behind, trying hard to stifle her laughter at the clueless expression on the nurse's face.

Over the next two days Steve made numerous trips by the desk, pushing a blanketed wheelchair, carrying an extra squirmy pile of bedding, pulling an overloaded laundry cart. No one ever questioned what the grinning man was up to.

The nurses were aware, however, of the improvement in Chipper. His face brightened, his eyes opened wider, his smile was more spontanious.

When Chipper was asleep for the night with Buddy stretched comfortably at his side, Sharron took the chance to voice some concerns.

"Steve, I'm worried. He's just not eating enough. I couldn't bear to have them re-attach that darned feeding tube."

"Have you tried all his favorites?" Steve suggested.

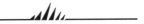

"That's part of the problem. His favorites aren't his favorites any more. Do you know what we finally got him to nibble on the other day? Tuna fish! Chipper hates—hated tuna! And when I told them to bring him root beer, his absolute favorite, he spit it out as fast as it went in. He's lost twenty pounds, Steve. We've got to do something."

"Have you asked Chip what he'd like?"

"Of course . . . I mean . . . well," Sharron stammered to a stop. After a pause, she said sheepishly, "I didn't think to actually ask him what he wanted. He gets so frustrated when he can't find the right words. We can't serve him a *doctor*, you know."

Steve gave her a wry smile, then thought for a minute. "OK, let's make it a game, like Mr. Cantor does. We'll play twenty questions."

First thing the next morning, Steve sat on the bed and the games began. It wasn't long before the yes-and-no questions narrowed the conversation down to the fact that Chipper was hungry and he did want something to eat. Steve grew quite optimistic and asked frankly, "Chipper, what do you want to eat?"

To everyone's surprise, he blurted out, "Bouncy balls!"

"Bouncy balls? Bouncy balls. You heard the boy, Mum. Get him some bouncy balls."

Sharron began giggling.

"Yes," Chipper responded again: "Bouncy balls."

"Next question," Steve kept up the game. "What in the world are bouncy balls?" He looked at Sharron, and got a grinning shrug. Chipper shifted in his bed, wanting to communicate more. He began to look frustrated, and Sharron grew uneasy.

"Meatballs?" she quickly offered.

Chipper's face told her that was not it.

"Doughnut holes?" Steve called out.

Chipper shook his head emphatically.

"Peas? Grapes? Popcorn?" Steve was on a roll. "Potatoes? Ice cream?"

Chipper looked to his mother.

"Oranges? Apples? Peaches?" she ventured.

"I know!" Steve jumped back in. "Lemonheads? Pom Poms? Nerds? M&M's? Aaaa . . . 7-up?"

"7-up?" Sharron gave him a quizzical look.

"You know, the fizz!" Steve defended himself. "It looks like bouncy balls to me."

The two of them began laughing. But Sharron suddenly stopped and jumped up. "I've got it! I've got it! Tapioca pudding!"

Steve was ready for more guffaws, but Chipper sat up tall and yelled, "Yes! Bouncy balls!"

"He had some the other day," Sharron explained. "But he used to hate the stuff. I just didn't think . . . Holy Toledo, Chipper! You did it. You just ordered yourself some breakfast."

18

Pretty Good

REHAB

If the key to Chipper's progress was doing the right thing at the right moment, somehow that key had been turned. Chipper was moving forward in ways no one would have imagined possible three weeks earlier. Mark Cantor wanted his parents to see what strides he and Chipper had been making.

Chipper

"When we get to my office," he whispered to Steve, "ask Chipper how he's feeling."

As soon as they were seated, Steve gave his son a pat and asked, "So Chip, how are you feeling today?"

"Pretty good," Chipper replied, without the slightest hesitation.

"He answered you!" Sharron exclaimed. The smiling faces told her they were all in on something. "OK, let me give it a try. Chipper, what would you like to do today?"

"Pretty good," he said again, grinning.

"I'll give you a hint, Sharron." Mr. Cantor leaned forward. "Make the questions simple."

"Gotcha. Chipper, are you having a good day?"

"Yes," Chipper responded, glancing over at Mark, who gave him a nod of encouragement.

Sharron was delighted. She clapped her hands as Steve joined in.

"Do you want to go back to your room, Chip?"

Again the glance toward Mark.

"No," he replied.

Steve gave a thumbs up. "Way to say it, Champ!"

"Pretty good," Chipper grinned.

"Pretty good is right!" Sharron laughed. "Mr. Cantor, you're a miracle worker."

"If there are miracles, it's Chipper who's working them," he answered. "By the way, your son calls me *Mark*. I think it's time you did."

Steve and Sharron stood to leave, but Chipper was not through with the surprises. He put his dog on the floor and motioned for his dad to stand across the room. Slowly he rose from his chair, took a moment to balance himself, and started walking. Face aglow, he shuffled one foot forward, then the other, inching across the floor until he had walked the full length of the room. He nearly tackled his dad when he reached him.

Steve gave him a bear hug and shouted, "All right!" as Sharron jumped up to join them.

"You are awesome, Chipper!" She cried.

"Pretty good," he agreed.

"I think he's just showing off for his dad—or his dog," Mark teased, but his face beamed his delight.

"I just wish we could both stay longer," Steve said, nodding to where Buddy stood wagging away, looking up at Chipper.

"So do I," Mark said. "But I'm afraid we're pushing things as it is. Buddy will have to be a secret weekend guest only." He scratched behind the floppy brown ears. "Either that, or we'll have to hire him on as a staff therapist." Buddy wagged harder and started panting, as if he liked the idea.

That afternoon when Chipper's grandpa called, Sharron put Chipper on the phone for the first time since the accident. He did so well with his four-word vocabulary that when Sharron got back on the line her dad said, "There's not a thing wrong with that boy. What have you been worrying about?"

Turning to look at her son lying on the bed, tapping his foot to the music in Scotty's Walkman, she almost believed it herself.

"Well, Dad," she said, "it's nice to know he can fool some of the people some of the time. The truth is we've still got a long way to go. But we're getting there step by step. Word by word."

The next morning Chipper convinced Dr. Walker he was ready to have his IVs removed. The doctor let Chipper pull the tube, which he did with pleasure, calling out "pretty good" as he waved the disconnected end. Free at last from all his tubes and attachments, Chipper reached for his Utah Jazz shirt and pulled it over his head. He plopped on his All Stars cap and gave an automatic flip of the bill to wear it catcher's style.

"Wow! Don't you look handsome." Sharron applauded her son's first successful effort to dress himself. Today he wasn't wasting any time. He had a party to go to.

He'd had enough of his wheelchair, too, and insisted on walking to the Rec. Room. Arm in arm, he and his mum scuffled down the hall like Dorothy and the Scarecrow en route to the Emerald City. All that was missing were the magic bubbles which Chipper saw to the minute he sat down. Flurries soon floated amid balloons and streamers as the room filled with party guests. When Tug was wheeled in, Sharron jumped up to greet him.

"Look at you! You're looking better every day, guy." Tug lifted his chin and came out with a word that made Sharron draw back in shock. His mother quickly explained.

"Remember when Chipper was stuck on the word *doctor*? Unfortunately, Tug somehow got stuck on . . . that word you just heard. I never imagined I'd be glad to hear him say *that*, but we're just thrilled he's talking."

Pretty Good

When Debbie wheeled Bryn into the room, everyone let out three cheers for the guest of honor. Bryn was going home. After seven years of corrective surgeries, her back was finally strong enough to support her weight. Fused, braced, and wrapped, she was ready to learn to walk and face the real world.

Sharron tried to smile as she handed Debbie the going-away card she'd made. "You'll never know how much you've strengthened me. It won't be the same here without you." Trying to lighten things up, she added, "Now maybe Chip and I will have a chance at winning a wheelchair race in the garden."

Dr. Tait and her therapists were starting games on the rug, Rehab's own special versions of spin the bottle, hot potato, pin-the-tail, and musical wheelchairs. They sang "B-i-n-g-o," clapping, rapping, or stomping personalized rhythms to the beat. When it was time to decorate the cup-cakes, Sharron watched Chipper wobble to the counter with the rest of the excited kids.

"A party is a party," she thought and sat back to drink in the delightful sounds of children having fun.

The next day Chipper had a surprise celebration of his own.

"We have a tradition here in physical therapy," Warren said, escorting Chipper to the walking pad. "When you can walk this pad without the bars, like you've been doing, you've earned a special reward." He handed him a Nerf basketball and hoop. "You're on the team, Champ. Wanna try a shot?"

Chipper

Chipper stepped back, focusing on the rim like there was nothing else in the world. Every time the ball missed and bounced away, he would limp to it, pick it up, and shoot again. He kept it up until, finally, he hit one.

"You'd better put the Jazz on notice." Warren laughed. "They have a shooter in the wings."

While Chipper and Sharron taped the Nerf hoop to the hall wall, a new boy, Johnny, moved in next door. Sharron couldn't guess his age by looking at him. Beneath the criss-crossing straps that harnessed him in the wheelchair, his body almost disappeared. He was so small and thin—like a six-year-old. But his arms and legs seemed to go on for-ever, like a lanky teenager. His hands were curled, white and frail, and his feet twisted and limp. He didn't say a word, but flashed Chipper a winning smile as an elderly couple pushed him past and into Bryn's old room.

Sharron gave them a few minutes to get settled, then introduced herself. Johnny's mother explained that his natural parents put him up for adoption when they learned he had muscular dystrophy.

"That's when we got him. He's the joy of our life," Mrs. Benson told her. "But the state wouldn't let us adopt him. Some ridiculous policy about foster parents not being al-lowed to adopt. When we made a little fuss, they took him away from us—nearly broke our hearts. And where did they put him? In some generic institution where no one even knew him, because they couldn't find another family that wanted him."

"Now, Mother," Mr. Benson cut in. "Mrs. Mangum did-n't ask for our whole life history."

"No, please. I want to hear the rest," Sharron insisted.

"I do tend to run on. But it's just so . . . wrong the way some silly laws are set up. We love this boy. Yet we were denied custody."

"But you ended up with him?"

"Finally, after we sued. Sold everything we had and mortgaged our farm to pay legal costs. But he's ours now. And we're so excited about his new computerized wheelchair."

"About what?"

"They've developed this incredible wheelchair that will even talk for him. We're here so he can learn to use it. Just imagine, for the first time in years Johnny's going to be able to really talk to us. All he has to do is learn to type the words, and the chair will do the rest. He's as smart as a whip. His disease just won't let his mind tell his body what to do anymore." She beamed at Johnny, who had pushed himself into the hallway to watch Chipper shoot hoops.

Chipper shuffled over to Johnny's side and dropped the ball into his lap, then looked across the hall to the taped-up backboard. Johnny smiled his awesome smile, squeezed the foam ball between his wrists, lifted with all his might, and let it fly. Looping high, it sailed across the hallway and bounced off the rim.

"Yes!" Chipper squealed. Limping his way across the hall, Chip picked up the ball, backed up and shot. He got some speed on it this time, but the ball missed the hoop, ricocheted off the wall, and plopped smack in the middle of a food tray parked one door down. Leftover green jello splatted onto the wall and a plastic spoon flipped up and over in the air . . . somersaulting its way right into a half empty glass of milk.

Plink!

The sound seemed to echo all the way down the hall before Chipper looked out of the corner of his eye at Johnny. Both his gangly arms were stretched high in the air, signaling a three-pointer! The boys burst into laughter and Chipper attempted a jubilant jump.

"Yes!" he called. "Pretty good!"

19

Outside World

"Chipper! Guess who's coming down the hall?"

Chipper gave his mother a blank look.

"Do you remember who I said was coming today? Think hard."

He stared hard at his mother's face for a few moments. She let him take his time, unsure whether he was trying to compute the question or remember who was coming. Then a light touched his eyes.

"Doctor," he said. Chip flopped his arms to his lap, scowled, and let out a deep breath. It was obvious the word wasn't the one he wanted.

"Good try, Chip. It's Dad, and he brought Scotty and Terie." Sharron busied herself tidying up the room as she spoke. "Just watch the door. I can hear them coming." She was straightening a chair by the door when around the corner popped the mischievous face of a toy monkey. She jumped back with a startled squeal that made Chipper laugh. Steve poked his head inside the door, next to the monkey.

"Today's test: which one is the monkey and which one is the daddy?" He stepped in and tossed the monkey on the bed in front of his son, who was smiling as wide as his face would allow. "How's my tree-killer today?"

"Pretty good!" Chipper said with giggling enthusiasm. He snatched up the monkey and held it out in front of him, grinning at the silly face that stared back.

"Pretty good, huh? That's the best news I've heard in weeks!" Steve gave the monkey a rap on the head. "Know what this is, Chip? It's a monkey. A toy monkey. How would you like to see a real one today?"

Sharron turned from the sink where she was filling a water picture. "Don't tell me you're sneaking monkeys in now!" she laughed.

"Actually, I was thinking of sneaking us out. How does a trip to the zoo sound?"

"The zoo? Do you think he's up . . . I'm not sure whether Doctor Tait . . . " Sharron stammered.

"I can always tell when I'm being talked about." Dr. Tait was in the doorway.

"How? Does your nose itch?" Steve reached to shake the doctor's hand.

"No. It's usually a more direct clue, like the sound of my name filtering down the hall."

"Good morning, Doctor." Sharron smiled up at her. "We were discussing Steve's latest scheme. He's talking about sneaking out of here and taking this boy to the zoo. What do you think of that?"

"I just thought it would be easier than sneaking the zoo in here," Steve said, raising his eyebrows up and down.

That image was enough to trigger a belly laugh from Scott. Chipper, realizing something funny was going on, joined in with his brother for the pure pleasure of it.

"I think he's serious, Doc." Sharron spoke up. The humor wasn't enough to erase her fearful thoughts. "Would it really be . . . safe?"

"For Chipper or the animals?" Steve winked.

"Be serious, Steve. I want to know what the doctor thinks."

Steve wiped the smile from his face with his hand and focused his attention on Dr. Tait.

"Right now we are trying to stimulate Chipper in as many ways as we can. I can't think of a better place to do that than a zoo, can you?"

"Nope!" Steve responded with the enthusiasm of someone whose team had just been joined by a star athlete.

"Opportunity for stimulation—and germs." Sharron was still unconvinced.

"Don't worry, Sharron. His body is so full of antibiotics right now, a germ wouldn't have a fighting chance. Not even an elephant germ. Besides, he's got to re-enter the world sooner or later. In fact, that's what I was on my way to talk with you about."

Now the doctor really had their attention.

"In last night's staff meeting we all agreed that barring any major change we can probably release Chipper by the end of next week, after the Fourth of July traffic dies down."

The whole room went still as her words sunk in.

"Home?" Sharron finally asked. "You mean . . . take him home?" Not knowing if she was going to laugh or cry, Sharron sank to her chair. She couldn't count the times she'd dreamed of this day, but now, the thought of caring for Chipper at home alone sent ice water through her veins.

"Sounds like you're outvoted, Mom. We're going to the zoo!" Scotty jumped back to the subject, unaware of what his mom was feeling.

"You'd like to go with us to the zoo, wouldn't you Chipper?" Terie asked.

Chipper gave a nod of his head, then looked down at the monkey on his lap, as if waiting for its opinion. Terie took up the grinning plaything and became its voice.

"Oh boy! The zoo! Yippee!" She tossed it in the air. It did a swan dive, then landed upside down beside Chipper, whose expression of glee was as exuberant as the monkey's.

The sun was noon-warm in a cloudless sky when the Mangum family pulled into the parking lot of Hogle Zoo. They pushed through the squeaky turn-bar and into the park. Reaching the head of the maze of paths, Sharron paused. The rest of her family was already headed for the lion cages when she called to them.

"Steve! Don't you think Chipper needs a wheelchair? He hasn't been walking on his own that long."

"Appears to me he's doing just fine," Steve called back, gesturing toward the kids. The three of them were skittering up the zoo trail toward the cages, arms linked, laughingly oblivious to their parents' distractions. Sharron watched as Steve trotted to catch up with them.

"We're just a normal family at the zoo," she told herself, trying to believe the words. But a voice in her whispered, "You've got to watch him every minute. You don't know what could happen. Something could go wrong any time. Watch him . . . watch him . . . "

Nothing did go wrong. The day sailed by, so smooth and delightful that Sharron herself began to believe they were getting back to normal.

The doctor had been right; Chipper loved the excitement of the zoo. Wide-eyed and silent, he watched the polar bear lumber over the rocky ledge and bellyflop into the pool. Her cubs followed close behind, rolling and wrestling in a growly knot, until the splashing water gave them an unexpected shower and sent them squealing and tumbling back up the hill. Scott got his brother to reach out and let the elephant search his hand for goodies with her trunk. Barely batting an eye, Chipper stood as still as a statue until the elephant blew air and slime all over his palm.

"Aghh!" He cried out, wiping his hand on his pants. When Chipper turned to stare down the beast for its bad manners, even Sharron couldn't help laughing.

The high point was the monkeys. Watching the frenzied antics of a treeful of them, Chipper laughed until he was red in the face. He squealed and giggled as they jumped and chattered from limb to limb. Every now and then one would come around, curiously eyeing Chipper with its round, black eyes. After the experience with the elephant, Chip wasn't about to let it too close, so he'd clap his hands and stomp his feet to send the monkey back to its monkey business.

He was making good use of his camera, with the help of his brother and sister. They spent the afternoon snapping pictures of animals from every angle. Scotty snapped a quick one of Chipper grinning from ear to ear as he hugged Elsie the Cow. Cow or giraffe, all held the same fascination for Chipper. For him, this was a brand new world.

As they drove back down the interstate toward Primary Children's, the kids grew suddenly quiet, reluctant for the fun to end. On an impulse, Steve turned south and parked beneath a neon banner that flashed "49th Street Galeria."

"I don't know about you guys, but I could go for some pinball!" Steve's eyes sparkled as the cheers of approval sounded. He studied his wife's face. "Don't worry, we won't stay long."

Sharron struggled again with her anxieties. When the group stepped up to the batting cage, her concerns grew stronger. How would Chipper feel, watching Scotty whack each ball right on the mark? Could he take the disappointment when he attempted it, and failed? Maybe Scotty would miss on purpose, so Chipper's expectations would not be so great. She looked at Scotty, bat raised over his shoulder in anticipation and eyes pinned to the pitching machine. Miss on purpose? Not Scotty. He hit every ball that flew at the bat.

Then he stepped back and handed the bat to Chipper. Sharron started forward, but Steve caught her eyes with a look that said, let him go, Mum. She watched Chipper mimic his brother. He set his feet, raised the bat high, and focused on the machine. Scotty discretely switched the lever to slow speed and put in a quarter. Sharron was preparing a speech in her head as she watched . . . "Nice try, Chipper! It doesn't matter if you don't hit them, as long as you —" Her thoughts were split by the *thwack!* of Chipper's bat hitting the first ball. The family cheered so loudly that people stopped and heads turned to see what amazing feat had taken place.

"He hit the ball!" Steve cried out to a puzzled passerby. "My boy! He hit the ball!" Jumping up and down, he ran over to Chipper and nearly knocked him down with a proud father's shoulder-slap and hug. Sharron's eyes shone with tears of elation as she watched the joy on Chipper's face.

In celebration of Chipper's accomplishment the family stopped at a nearby restaurant for dinner. "It'll be good for

Chipper

Chipper to have this experience," Steve told Sharron as they turned into the House of Pancakes parking lot. "Let's see how he does."

Chipper looked long and hard at the menu. Sharron sensed his discomfort. It was something deeper than confusion, a certain melancholy that troubled her. She watched him for a while, then caught his eye.

"What is it, Chipper? Do you know what you want?"

Chipper looked deep into his mother's eyes, then ran his finger up and down the page.

"I . . . I . . . " He struggled to find and form the words. His family stopped talking now and all eyes were on him.

"I . . . I . . . doctor." He slammed shut the menu and threw it to the floor.

"It's OK, Chipper," his mom reassured. "It will come. Try again." Chipper breathed deep.

"I . . .can't . . ." He reached down, picked up the menu, and ran his finger over the words again.

"Read. Is that what you want to tell us, Chipper? You can't read?" Terie's voice was tender.

"Yes. Read." Chipper whispered the words.

Sharron leaned in, her eyes fixed firm and steady on his. "Chipper, listen closely to me. Remember when you couldn't walk?"

Chipper nodded.

"It took some time, but you worked hard. Now you can walk. Today you walked through the zoo. We're all so proud of you!" She leaned back in the booth, still looking into Chipper's eyes, and promised: "You will learn."

20

Dr. Sunshine

"Happy Fourth of July, dear Chipper,
Happy Fourth of July to you!"

Chipper sat up in bed, surrounded by a circle of smiling
faces. His family was all there. Paula and Tina had come
from ICU along with BarDonna, Johnny, and other friends

from Rehab. Tina stepped forward to fuzz the new hair poking like whiskers from Chip's head.

"Hey kid, you look pretty good with hair," she funned. Then with a matador's flair she swept from behind her back a box wrapped in shiny yellow paper, with a huge rainbow-striped bow on top.

"Well, aren't you going to open it?" BarDonna asked.

Chipper's uncertain glance at his mom said, "What do I do now?" She nodded a smiling go-ahead, and Chipper reached for the bow, then hesitated, uncertain whether he should spoil the pretty package.

"Go ahead, Hon. Open it."

Chipper gave the ribbon a puny pull, then looked to see if he was in trouble. Everyone cheered, so he let loose and went after the paper.

He fumbled to remove the lid and get a peek inside. His eyes opened wider and again he froze.

"You can take it out. It's for you."

With great care, Chipper lifted from the tissue a small porcelain figurine—a little boy, dressed up like a doctor. BarDonna came forward and cupped her hands around Chipper's as he held the delicate statue.

"For our own Dr. Sunshine," she declared. "That's you, Chipper. It's our way of thanking you for taking such good care of the children here. You're just like a doctor, giving out your own bubbly sunshine medicine. From now on we're calling you Dr. Sunshine. How do you like that?"

Chipper ran his fingers along the delicately colored form of the boy. Yellow hair poked out in childlike disarray from beneath the doctor's hat, and his clear, sky-blue eyes looked almost real against the cream-colored skin. His feet sported a pair of man-sized shoes, standing in a field of pastel flowers.

No one spoke as Chipper took his time examining his treasure. Finally he looked up.

"Pretty good," he said, triggering a peal of laughter.

As they were about to leave, Chipper handed the statue to his mother and started getting out of bed.

"Now, where are you off to?"

"Bubbles," Chipper exclaimed, and another round of laughter ensued as a pathway was cleared.

"Make way, Dr. Sunshine's making his rounds," Paula announced.

Chipper passed through, eagerly on his way, his dad and mother at his heels. He paused at the door to scoop a handful of suckers from his private collection of treats. They had just disappeared around the corner when Dr. Walker and Dr. Tait stopped in.

"I'm sorry, but Dr. Sunshine is way ahead of the two of you," BarDonna grinned as the others giggled. "He's off working miracles with his own kind of medicine."

"It's bubble time, huh?" Dr. Tait smiled. "Well, that's as good for these kids, I think, as just about anything we do. Not to mention what it does for Chipper."

"Double therapy, I'd say," Dr. Walker agreed.

"No," Dr. Tait corrected. "It's better than that. It's double-bubble therapy."

Scott and Chipper took turns clearing traffic while Johnny maneuvered his hot new wheelchair through the halls and elevators and out to the front lawn.

"Watch out!" Scott called when Johnny hit the wrong lever and sent his wheelchair speeding like a bumper car toward the back of an unsuspecting nurse. Managing a right turn just in the nick of time, Johnny saved the nurse from a double-decker ride down the hall on his lap.

"Excuse us, Miss," Scott apologized. "They should've equipped this rig with an air horn."

It wasn't the only near miss of the evening. The halls were filled with children, families, and nurses heading outdoors for the July Fourth fireworks. Though Johnny's driving was improving, in tight quarters like this no one was really safe. As the three boys finally came to a halt on the hospital lawn, Johnny let out a sigh of relief.

"Good show, John!" Scott patted his friend on the back. "We're here, we're alive, and you didn't get ticketed, even when you laid that rubber on the second floor." The feat was solemnized by slapping high fives.

"I'll tell you what Johnny, you take a break and Chip and I will go get the goods." Scott was eyeing the snack-laden table on the cafeteria patio like a hungry hawk. So while Chipper and his brother headed to the feast, Johnny put on his brakes and leaned back to take in the view.

It was a "glorious Fourth," as his adopted dad would put it. The air still hung heavy from the heat of the day. But if he sat still and thought about it he could feel a whisper of a breeze spilling down from Emigration Canyon. The sky was that rich, deep blue you only get to see just before it's too dark to tell its real color, and the stars were popping out faster than he could count. Wheeling to face the west, Johnny searched near the dusky horizon for Venus, his wishing star.

"Did you find it, Son?" Johnny's dad was behind him, as he had been so many evenings in Idaho. No one appreciates the cool of a summer's eve quite like a farmer. Ever since Johnny had joined his family Mr. Benson had carried or wheeled him to the back lawn to enjoy the richness of the sunset or to make a wish on the first star. On stormy nights they'd sit under the porch and watch the snow or rain fall to the earth—sometimes, they would go right out and sit in it. But they always made a wish. Johnny smiled his ear-to-ear grin that said he'd found his star and made his wish.

"Me too," his dad winked back. "Say, would ya look at that. Appears to me your wish is coming true."

Johnny turned to see Scott making his way across the lawn juggling three plates piled high with cookies and cakes of every description: chocolate chip, sugar, peanut butter, Oreo, and Johnny's favorite, fudge brownies. Chipper was worming his way behind his brother at a snail's pace, concentrating to balance three glasses of punch.

"Looks like we're just in time." Steve reached out to snitch a snickerdoodle from Scott's plate.

"Hey! The table's that way," Scott said, defending his booty. "This stuff's spoken for." By the time Sharron and Mrs. Benson had served up a few more plates of goodies, Scott was ready for more and Johnny had almost cleared his plate. Chipper hardly touched his, but Sharron

Chipper

wouldn't let Scott at it, so he headed back to the table for a second round. They spread a couple of quilts on the lawn and everyone settled back to wait for the big show. Except Chipper. With Buddy at his heels, he was making bubble rounds again.

When the first report boomed, Chipper almost lost his bubbles. He latched hold of his dog and made a beeline for his mom.

"It's the fireworks, Chip. Pretty loud, huh?"

"Pretty loud, huh!" Chipper squeezed between his mom and dad and nuzzled Buddy close.

The hillside echoed with the cracking, popping, and rumbling of fireworks, and with the rhythmic grandeur of classical music broadcast over radios. The sky was splintered with screaming colors: red, blue, shimmering white. Squeals of children's laughter burst like flares of joy with each blazing eruption. As the powerful finale filled the valley with exploding light and strains of *The Star Spangled Banner*, Chipper snuggled in close to his mom and put his hand on his heart.

It was a "glorious Fourth."

21

Setback

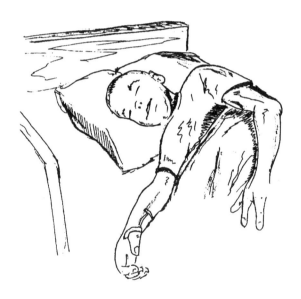

"Just six more days, Champ, and I'll take you home with me. We'll give you a couple of days rest, then on July 14th we'll be sitting at Aspen Mirror Lake reeling in trout." Steve pleaded with his son, who had him crunched in one of his famous headlocks. The grip wasn't loosening, and Steve waved his free hand at his wife for help.

Chipper

"You want to go home with Dad don't you Chipper?" Sharron asked.

"Dad!" he yelled through tears.

"I know you miss Daddy, Chip. But you need a few more days with Mark then Dad will come take you home. Now let Dad go, Honey."

Knowing he'd lost, Chipper released his hold. But he turned his back to his parents and started pouting.

"Come on, Son. How about walking your old dad to the car?"

Flopping onto his bed, Chip shot an angry look back, then pulled the quilt over his face. All Steve could do was give the lump in the bed a pat and tell it he loved it. He gave Sharron a hug and whispered, "I'll be glad when these good-byes are all behind us. I don't know who they're tougher on, him or me."

"Or me," Sharron thought. Out loud she said, "Maybe this will be the last one."

The thought churned up a quagmire of emotions. She missed the comfortable confusion of having the family under one roof, their constant coming and going, crazy plans hatching. She missed her own kitchen and home-cooked meals. Still, the thought of taking care of Chipper at home was far from comforting. She felt safe here where people knew how to care for her son. Here people understood. They knew his limits, his triumphs, small and great. At home, she wasn't so sure. Bubbles would lose some of their magic at Cedar Middle School. She looked at Chipper hiding beneath his covers and considered joining him there.

"Sharron," Steve took her hand. "Are you OK?"

Setback

"I was just thinking about going home. It makes me nervous. I don't know if I can take care of him. "

Steve put his other hand over hers and looked her in the eyes. "You talk like everything will be on your shoulders. That kind of thinking will wear you down, Sharron. Do me a favor, will you? This week, practice letting go. You've had so much to worry about, I think it's becoming a habit. It's time to focus on the positive. Wednesday, July 11, we're taking our son home. It's a dream come true. Now give me a smile so I can go in peace."

Sharron offered the smile. "OK, go home and start hunting up worms. I'll try to focus on next Saturday's family fishing trip."

But it was hard to think of fishing next Saturday when therapy right now demanded full attention. Chipper wasn't in the mood to concentrate or cooperate. It ended up another "let's try again tomorrow" visit, shortened by Chipper's sour mood. Physical therapy was no better.

When mealtime came Chipper refused to touch his food. Sharron dropped exhausted into a chair as the sun was dimming and looked at her son. He lay listless, a glazed expression settled across his face. She realized he was as tired and discouraged as she was, maybe more. Hoping to cheer him, she reached for the bubble jar.

"How about it, Chip. Let's start the bubble rounds. We could all use some fun."

Chipper only stared ahead. When BarDonna appeared, Sharron couldn't help but voice her concerns.

"I promised Steve I'd stop worrying about every little thing, but Chipper's been acting strange. He's been cross and irritable all day, and tonight he's almost incoherent. I have a feeling something's wrong."

BarDonna lay a hand on his cheek. "He's probably just a bit weary from the weekend, or he's missing his dad."

When he refused to brush his teeth, BarDonna tried to do it for him.

"My goodness, Dear. No wonder you didn't want supper," she gasped. "Sharron, come look at this poor boy's gums. They look like raw hamburger. I'll bet it's that darned Dilantin!"

"What?"

"His seizure medication. He may be having a reaction to it. I'm calling Dr. Tait."

Within minutes they were drawing blood for tests. Chipper didn't even complain, just turned over and went to sleep.

Friday morning Chipper woke up dizzy and sick to his stomach. After seeing results from the blood tests Dr. Tait gave Chipper a thorough examination.

"Well Chip, I guess I was wrong about the elephant germ," she said, pulling up a chair by his bed. "It looks like you've picked up a great big flu bug. And you're probably swallowing blood from those inflamed gums." She turned to Sharron. "I'm taking him off Dilantin, ordering Tegretol until the gums clear up." She gave Chipper's knee a pat. "Looks like you'd better take the day off. But don't get too comfortable. You've got patients out there who count on their daily visits from Dr. Sunshine."

As she left Sharron followed her into the hall.

Setback

"Do you think it's just a twenty-four-hour bug? Steve's really counting on taking him home next week."

"I hope so, Sharron. We'll watch him for a day or two and see how things go. Steve may have to be patient for a few extra days. I don't want to send him home until I'm sure he's ready."

Chipper slept most of the day while nurses and doctors filed in and out. When BarDonna came on duty, she watched him like a hawk.

"Maybe it's a forty-eight-hour bug," Sharron said, trying to stay calm. "Steve's going to be proud of me when he finds out I saw Chipper through this without panicking and calling."

"You're doing fine, Mom," BarDonna said, giving her a squeeze. "Hopefully he'll wake up tomorrow feeling a bit more . . . *chipper*."

He didn't. Tossing and turning through most of the night, neither Chipper nor Sharron slept. When the early sun streamed onto his bed, Chipper pulled a pillow over his head and whimpered with pain.

Sharron rushed to him. "What is it, Chipper?" Kneeling at his bedside, she removed the pillow. His skin looked gray and sallow. When he opened his eyes, they were sunken, dull and lifeless.

"Head . . . " he groaned, pulling the blanket back over his eyes. "Hurt." Sharron ran for a nurse.

Dr. Tait ordered a CAT scan, a spinal tap, and more blood tests. The stomachache was troubling, but the dizziness and headaches were what really worried her. The tests did nothing but eliminate a few possibilities: it was not influenza or infection in the brain. But exactly what it was they didn't know.

Sharron sat in the dark room with Chipper through the rest of the day, trying to write a little and crochet a little, trying to keep herself from calling Steve.

"He said he'd call tonight," she kept reminding herself. "Maybe by then I'll have good news for him. I can wait that much longer."

She made the bubble rounds herself, explaining to the children that Chipper would be back soon. They were upset and worried. Johnny made at least five visits during the day, checking on his friend. Jessie and Josie brought Tug in with them, but the visits drew no response from Chipper. Even a visit from Karl Malone, John Stockton, and Mark Eaton of the Utah Jazz failed to get a reaction from Chipper. He just wasn't up to visitors. Sharron thanked them for coming by and hung the autographed poster by Chipper's Nerf hoop, assuring them he'd love it when he got feeling better.

When Steve's phone call came Sharron did her best to sound calm.

"They're not really sure what the problem is yet. Dr. Tait's beginning to think it might be food poisoning. She said it's not unusual for brain trauma victims to get very ill when they pick up a bug. It doesn't take much to throw their whole system off balance when their body has gone through so many changes."

"Do you need me to come, Sharron?"

This was a real test. "No, no." She took a deep breath. "We're all expecting him to start feeling better any time now. Besides, I know you'll want to take next week off, when he comes home. We're doing fine."

"I guess we'll just wait this out then. Let me know if there are any changes. And tell Chipper I've got his tackle box ready."

As Sharron hung up the phone, she shook out her trembling hands.

"We are doing fine," she repeated under her breath. "Just fine."

By Monday the air was tense. Since Chipper's room was the last one before the therapy center, everyone who passed by stopped to check on him. Some of the younger children cried when Chipper didn't blow bubbles for them. The toughest visitor for Sharron to deal with was Johnny. Half the morning he sat beneath the basketball hoop and tried to say Chipper's name. He wanted to surprise his best friend, hoping it would help him get better. During therapy many of the children made "Get well soon Dr. Sunshine" cards and dropped them off on the way back to their rooms.

Chipper wasn't improving. By 5:00 P.M., Dr. Tait ordered an IV.

"Hopefully you won't need this for long, Champ. But we need to get some food into you somehow."

"No . . . " Chipper's voice was weak. He struggled to keep from having the tube reinserted. By the time the ordeal was over he was gulping air between sobs, barely able to breathe. While Dr. Tait and Warren worked on Chipper, BarDonna put her arm around Sharron and took her from the room.

"Come with me, Dear. You're shaking in your boots."

Sharron clung to her arm. "I just wish someone could tell me what's gone wrong. He was doing so well."

Two more days dragged by. Chipper was poked, scoped, and tested until Sharron felt she'd been through a crash course in diagnosis. Still no answers. When all available options had been exhausted at Primary Children's, Dr. Tait suggested taking Chipper to LDS Hospital for an MRI.

"A what?" Sharron asked.

"A scan that will give us detailed pictures of his brain. We're thinking his headaches and dizziness could be a result of small seizure activity or some other problem our equipment isn't picking up. Perhaps some debris we missed in surgery, a blood clot, even a tumor. We're hoping the MRI can give us some new direction."

Chipper and Sharron were loaded into an ambulance and whisked across town for a high-tech photo session that took most of the afternoon.

Exhausted from strain and unrelenting pain, Chipper slept until early dawn Wednesday morning—the day they had planned to take him home.

Sharron stirred in her restless sleep. Vaguely, she heard BarDonna talking softly in the dimly lit room. It didn't take long to realize she was praying.

"My Lincoln, he lived to experience many wonderful things. But Chipper here, he's so young. He has so much yet to learn . . . so much to offer. Let him live . . . "

In her silent heart, Sharron added her own pleas. "You spared him once before . . . don't take him now."

Setback

Immediately the image of her son grimacing in pain engulfed her. A pang of guilt hit.

"Am I thinking only of myself? I just want my son to be free from this trial. Please strengthen him . . . and me . . . to accept Thy will."

Sharron felt a whisper of peace. Her prayer became a psalm of gratitude for the many loving, healing hands who cared for her son. BarDonna slipped quietly from the room.

Watching the hands on the clock make their tedious circles, Sharron waited for Dr. Tait to come with a report from yesterday's MRI. Except for blood tests every three hours, they were letting Chipper rest. He was so dizzy and in such pain that sleep was his only escape.

Sharron attempted some escape of their own, scooting her chair near the window and cracking the curtain for enough light to read by. But escape was not easy. She finally gave up, closed the book and her eyes, and tried to clear her mind. Just then Chipper started tossing his head. Her eyes popped open. His bed began to shake. Thinking he was having a nightmare, Sharron scrambled to wake him. By the time she reached his side, Chipper's entire body was jerking. His eyes rolled in his head and his mouth pulled and twisted to one side. The whole bed began to bump and jolt. Sharron stood frozen.

"Nurse . . . " She could barely utter the word. "Nurse!" At last, on the third try, the word came out. The whole floor heard this time.

"Chipper! Can you hear me?" She was still screaming. "Wake up! Wake up!" All training she'd had about seizures flew from her mind; all she could do was try to keep him from falling off the bed. "Stop, Chipper! Stop! Please!" By the time a nurse came through the door, the convulsions had ended. But they couldn't wake him.

22

The Dream

"**M**um . . . Mum."

Sharron's eyes opened a crack. "Chipper?" She listened in the dark room. For half the night every squeak of a bed spring or sudden movement from Chipper brought panic. Haunted by the specter of another seizure, she barely allowed herself to sleep. When she did doze off, the vision of her son clutched in seizure tyrannized her dreams. Now, unsure if the voice she had heard was real or imagined, she just listened.

"It couldn't have been Chipper," she thought." The voice sounded too clear, too calm."

"Mum?" He called again.

This time Sharron leaned up on an elbow and whispered.

"Chipper? Are you awake?"

In the green shadowed light of the monitor Sharron found her way to Chipper's bed. He was patting the spot next to him, so she carefully moved the tubes and laid at his side.

"Love you, Mum," he said.

She reached an arm across his chest and snuggled closer. "I love you, Chipper."

Something about his words stirred uneasiness within her. She pondered in the quiet that followed. He was so calm, alert. A chill shivered through her. She had heard that often just before someone dies, they wake up to say goodbye.

"Are you all right, Son?"

"Pretty good."

Though his voice was still unusually clear, the familiar words were calming. Sharron gave him a squeeze and began rubbing his arm.

"What woke you?" she asked him.

"My angel." His voice was matter-of-fact, innocent.

The rubbing stopped. "You have an angel, Chipper? In your dream?"

The Dream

"Yes . . . watching."

"Did the angel talk to you?"

"Yes . . . no." Chipper paused. "I felt him . . . here." He moved his hand to his chest. "In me," he whispered.

Sharron lay still, unsure what to make of the dream her son was describing.

"What did he look like, Son?"

Chipper turned to her and rubbed the fingertips of both hands across his eyebrows. "Big," he said. His hands then spread to cover his cheeks.

"He had a beard? And big eyebrows?"

"Yes. Big."

"Do you know his name, Chipper?"

He sat still a moment, then shrugged his shoulders and shook his head. Yesterday, after the seizure, that much movement would have made Chipper violently ill. Again Sharron had to push down her fears. It all felt too unnatural. He was not the same sick boy of a few hours ago. She gathered her courage for the next question.

"Why did your angel come?"

She lay still, waiting. Again a shrug of his shoulders was his answer and she was left to wonder if he didn't know or if he couldn't tell her. Watching his face for a clue, she noticed the glimmer of a tear streak from the corner of his eye.

"Are you frightened, Son? Did the angel make you afraid?"

"No . . ." he smiled feebly. After a moment of silence, he spoke again, but this time she could barely hear him. "Tired," he whispered, and drifted off to sleep.

Chipper

Sharron held him close, measuring every breath he took, praying it was not his last.

Morning finally peeked through the edges of the curtains. Chipper was still breathing deeply. When BarDonna appeared Sharron told her what had happened in the night.

"Maybe he was remembering something from the past," she suggested. "With brain trauma, all kinds of images get mixed together and pop up. Maybe some good will come of it. At least it helped him relax."

"I don't want him this relaxed!" Sharron's reply was sharper than she intended. BarDonna turned to her.

"What's bothering you, Dear?"

Sharron's answer came with hesitation. "I'm afraid that this 'angel' has come to take him from me," she finally blurted. She studied BarDonna's face, half expecting to see disbelief. But her expression did not change; she only waited for Sharron to continue.

"BarDonna, if you had seen him last night. He was so peaceful. Too peaceful. Like he'd given up the fight. Beneath her breath she added, "and I don't blame him."

This time BarDonna reacted. "Now that's all I'm going to hear of that kind of talk," she scolded. "Sharron, your son has been diagnosed with vertigo. Dr. Tait can treat him for that. Right now he's feeling sicker than a dog, but he's going to get over it. *Chipper* is not the one giving up! I can tell you this, though. If that boy feels his own Mum giving up on him, why, then we're going to see a child who's given up the fight."

Sharron just sat there. It had been awhile since she'd had a tongue lashing like this and she wasn't quite sure how to take it. BarDonna let her stew for just a minute, then moved to her side.

"I think all you need is a shoulder to cry on. I'll make you a deal. When you get feeling like you've got to get this load off your heart for a while, you just ring that buzzer. These old shoulders are still pretty good for crying on. No one here expects you to carry this all on your own. But I don't want to hear any more talk about giving up. Not on our boy. Deal?"

Sharron looked into the face of this woman who had cared for Chipper like her own grandchild.

"Deal."

"Plus, I'm prescribing my own personal cure. I'll sit here with Chipper while you go get Marilyn Wood and treat her to a giant-sized slice of chocolate cake. I don't want to see you back here until you've eaten every crumb."

"For breakfast?"

"No arguing. Now scoot!"

Sharron fell asleep much easier that night. Maybe it was knowing Steve would arrive in the morning, and maybe it was just plain old exhaustion. Whatever it was, she hardly stirred until 4:00 A.M. when like a re-run of the night before, Chipper called out to her. With the same clear voice he summoned her to his side.

"Going home," he exclaimed. As he spoke she could see the light of excitement dancing in his eyes, even in the dark room. Chipper had never said the word *home* before and Sharron often wondered if he remembered any home but this.

"Going home! My turn."

Chipper

"Your turn for what, Chipper?" Sharron was shaking. "Is it your turn to go home . . . to heaven?"

"No. Go home to Dad." She'd been unconscious of the breath she was holding until it rushed from her lungs.

"Oh, Chipper, do you remember our home?"

"Yes." When he said it, she knew it was so. His voice was colored with longing, and she felt the tension release even more with his next words: "My angel . . . gone home too."

23

Tell Jason I Love Him

Sharron focused the camera and stepped back for a broader shot. Chipper lay peacefully on his bed, his arms wrapped around his dog. "Steve, step in close. I want to take one of the two of you before the nurse comes with another dose of antibiotic."

Chipper

"I think Buddy's his best antibiotic," Steve observed, grinning for the camera. The dog opened his eyes at the sound of his name and made a feeble attempt at a tail wag.

Sharron clicked the picture and sat beside her husband.

"And you're my best medicine. I think I've improved almost as much as Chipper in the past two days."

"I wish I didn't have to leave you alone again, but I'm afraid I've got to get back on the road. As for you, my Dear, you've earned a little R & R. How about a hot date? I know just the man, and he happens to have the morning free."

"It sounds great but I—"

"Good!" Steve broke in. "Then it's settled."

"How is he this morning?" Mark spoke from the doorway.

"Much better. He asked for jello last night, and kept it down. He's still sleeping most of the time, though," Sharron explained. "Doctor Tait said he needs as much rest as possible. You weren't planning on therapy this morning, were you?"

Mark grinned as he jotted on his notepad. "I know I'm pushy, but I can sure wait until the child is well."

"I didn't mean to sound—"

"Like a mother hen?" Steve finished.

"I understand." Mark smiled at Sharron. "He needs a mother hen. But we have lost a little ground. I'm anxious to get going again as soon as the time is right. I'll check back in the morning."

Mark had to side-step around Johnny's wheelchair as he was leaving.

"Good morning, Johnny!" Sharron welcomed him in.

But Johnny stayed in the doorway looking at Chipper, his brows knotted with concern.

"I think he's much better today. It won't be long before he's able to play with you again, I'm sure."

Johnny's face brightened.

"Come on in." Steve stood to offer his assistance, but Johnny waved and reversed his chair out the door.

"Was it something I said?" Steve chuckled, settling back in his chair.

A nurse's aide entered, rattling a breakfast tray.

"Oh, he's still asleep, huh? I was told to bring Chipper up a special breakfast. I guess they want something in his stomach, if you can get him to eat. But the nurse said not to push him. Just cheer him on and do the best you can." With an encouraging smile, she set the tray on the stand by the bed. "Oh, Sharron, you have a phone call."

"I'll take it at the nurse's station, so I won't disturb him," Sharron whispered to Steve. "If he stirs, see if he'll take some jello."

"Yes ma'am."

Sharron leaned across the counter and punched the flashing line. "This is Sharron."

"Mom? How's it going?" Terie's voice was cheery.

Sharron hesitated, weighing her words. She had not told the children about the seriousness of Chipper's sickness.

"Well, actually we've had a little setback. But Chipper's doing much better today."

"Setback? What do you mean?"

"After the outing Chipper became very ill, Terie. For awhile they didn't know what was happening. That's why

we put off bringing him home. He started having seizures and vomiting and—"

"Seizures? Mum, why didn't you tell us! When was this? After the zoo? That was a week ago!" Terie's words spilled out with sudden alarm.

"It's OK, Terie. He's much better today. His temperature is down and—"

"Temperature? What's going on? We've been telling people he was about ready to come home. He was doing so well."

"He is doing well, Terie. He's pulling through it."

"Oh come on Mum. It's not like I'm a five-year-old who can't take the truth.

"You're right, Terie. I should have told you. Maybe you'd better tell the others."

Sharron hung up the phone and leaned heavily on the counter.

"Are you all right?" It was Marilyn Wood. "You look pretty spent."

Sharron raised her head and attempted a smile. Marilyn drew closer and searched her face with concern. "What is it, Sharron? Anything I can do?"

Sharron let the words spill out. "I'm feeling a little lost. I can't seem to do anything right. I don't know when to hold on and when to let go. Chipper isn't the only one trying to find himself right now."

"I know what you're saying. I was looking at Wendy just now, wondering about her future, and if I can be the mother she needs. I'm really afraid of what's ahead. Matt has a brother who was head injured. We've watched him struggle . . . with people, and the way they treat him, think of him. From our point of view, it seems so hard. But he's happy and living a relatively normal life."

"Relatively normal." Sharron repeated the words, a distant look in her eyes. Then she seemed to snap back. She raised her face and looked Marilyn in the eyes. "You're pretty wonderful, Marilyn. Here you are, with a child still in a coma, and you're the one cheering me up."

Marilyn smiled and took her friend's hand. "And you'll be cheering me up tomorrow. But right now you'd better go get ready for your lunch date."

Steve was smiling as he steered into a parking lot.

"What are you up to now?" Sharron gave him a sideways glance. She realized there were other motives behind his innocent suggestion for "a hot date." He didn't answer, but pulled next to a row of shiny new boats and turned off the car. She waited for him to explain. But he took his time, enjoying her curiosity.

"Well, what do you think?" he finally said.

"I think you're trying to tell me something, and I'm not catching on. How about a hint."

"Just wanted your opinion. Do you like it?" Steve gestured towards a sleek blue-and-silver motor boat in front of them. Sharron followed his gaze.

"It's nice," she said.

"Let's get out and take a good look." Steve hopped out and skipped around to open Sharron's door, still grinning. They walked around the boat, Steve running his hand along the smooth chrome.

"Can you picture it? Cruising with the boys across that turquoise Lake Mead water, leaving a trail of foam like a jet in the sky, nothing to worry about but finding the best spot to drop our lines."

Watching him glow and dream, Sharron didn't speak her fears. "Won't that be wonderful" was what she said. "We'll never be back to the way we were" was what she was thinking.

"I'm really going to make up for lost time." Steve had the look of a man lost in a hopeful future. The sun was bright on his face as the visions filtered through his mind. He squinted under its rays, stepping back to admire the boat. "Well? Would you like to have a boat like this?"

"Sure. Someday."

"How about today?"

"Huh?"

"Do you really like it?"

"Sure, but—"

"Good, because it's ours. Ron Hunt gave it to us yesterday."

It was midafternoon when Steve and Sharron got back to the hospital. Steve was feeling pressed to get back to work, yet reluctant to wake his sleeping son and tell him he had to take Buddy and go. He was already much later getting off than he'd planned.

"Should I just sneak out with Buddy and let him sleep?"

"I'm afraid that would really upset him—waking up to find both his dad and his dog gone, without even a goodbye."

"Yeah, I guess it would.

"Steve, I've been thinking about Scotty and Jason. Are they OK?"

"It seems to me they're closer than ever. They're together a lot. It's like they want everyone to know they're still best friends, no hard feelings. But I think Jason is struggling. He blames himself. He hasn't said—"

"Is Jason mad?" It was Chipper. Steve went to the bedside and took his son's hand.

"He's not mad Chip, he's just—"

"I made Jason mad."

Sharron was so amazed at Chipper's efforts to reason she missed his message. Until she saw his eyes. They were filled with anguish.

"Chip," Steve's voice was gentle. "Do you remember what happened on the mountain? When the tree fell on you, Jason was the one who cut it down. He would do anything to change what happened. But he can't. If he's sad, that's why."

It was hard to tell if Chipper comprehended what his dad was telling him. He began softly stroking his dog, and several minutes went by before he spoke.

"Dad?"

"Yes, Son?"

"Tell Jason . . . I love him."

24

Going Home

"Chip, you're early. The party doesn't start until this afternoon." Warren jumped from the stool where he was hanging crepe paper streamers and tossed his roll of tape onto the table. Chipper scooped it up, shot a quick glance at Warren, and shuffle-hopped back out.

"Hey! Where are you going with my tape?" Warren ran to the door in time to see Chipper duck into his room without a backward glance.

Going Home

"What was that?" a grinning candy striper questioned.

"I've been robbed! I didn't know that kid could move so fast. At least he left my credit cards," Warren laughed, jokingly checking his wallet.

Chipper fanned through the newspaper until he came to the comics, then spread the colorful pages flat on the bed. He pulled the corners up around his Nerf hoop, wrapping and taping, wrapping and taping, until not a peek hole was left uncovered. He pulled a bright green bow from a potted plant and taped it to the package. Not quite satisfied, he added a big yellow one. Now for the final touch. He pulled out the card he'd been working on all morning. In big uneven letters it said: "To Johnny. You are a winner!"

Chipper stepped back to inspect his work. A twitch of a grin escaped before he headed out to return Warren's tape.

"If any more questions come up, don't hesitate to ask. Even after you get home, we want you to feel free to call. You have our number." Dr. Tait drew the meeting to a close as Sharron went over her list again. All week she'd written questions about Chipper's care:

> How soon do I call if he gets sick?
> Can I let him ride a bike?
> What if he won't eat?
> How soon can friends come over?
> What if he has no friends?

The closer July 23rd got the more nervous Sharron felt. The day that had seemed so distant was just around the corner now. Tomorrow morning she and Steve were going back to Cedar City—with Chipper. As she looked around the table at these men and women who had been like family for the last fifty-two days, she wished she could take them with her.

"Unless anyone has more to add, I suggest we adjourn," Dr. Tait's voice broke through Sharron's thoughts. The doctor looked one more time at Sharron, then Steve, then did a quick once-around-the-able. "I guess that's it then. We'll see you all at Chipper's party."

When the Mangums got back to their room, Chipper wasn't there.

"I thought you were going to stay with him, Scott," Sharron scolded. "How long has he been gone?" Scott looked up from the TV.

"Huh?"

"Where's your brother?" Steve took over.

"Oh. I told him he could go with Jesse and Josie. I think they went to Tug's room."

Tug's room was empty. Steve and Sharron tried Wendy's.

When Steve opened the door, he found the Thompsons there with Matt and Marilyn. But no boys.

"You'll never guess what happened!" Marilyn was immediately on her feet running to give Sharron a hug.

"She talked! Wendy talked! She looked at me and said 'Mama.' We sent the twins to tell you."

Sharron gave Marilyn a hug and whispered, "Oh Marilyn! That's marvelous!" Steve walked over, shook Matt's hand, then knelt beside Wendy. He gave her a little peck on the cheek and told her "Thanks. Thanks for the greatest going away present ever."

"Where's Chipper?" Matt asked. "He'll want to hear about this."

"That's what we came for." Steve stood back up and turned to Matt. "He's someplace with Tug and the twins. We were hoping you could tell us where they went."

"Last I knew they were with Warren," Tug's dad piped in. "But it's pretty quiet around here. I'm starting to wonder what they're up to. We'd better put out a warning: The Four Musketeers are on the loose."

The warning was a little late. When Sharron and Julie walked past the nurses' station looking for their boys, the duty nurse called out to them.

"If you're looking for Tug and Chipper, I think I can help. They should be coming off that elevator any moment with a police escort."

"What?" the two mothers cried at once.

Just then the elevator doors parted, revealing four guilty looking kids and one stern nurse. She herded them to the desk and plopped four plaster masks on the counter.

"It's not Halloween, you know" she said, turning sharply on her heel and marching back to the elevator. She pushed the button and stood at attention while the silver doors slid shut and transported her back to the third floor.

"We were just trying to have a little fun," Josie explained. "She didn't have to get all mad."

Jesse broke in to carry on their defense: "Warren helped us make these masks out of cast plaster, and we thought the kids upstairs would think they were cool. We weren't trying to scare anybody, but this little kid just started

screaming at the top of his lungs like he'd seen a mummy or something."

The nurse started smiling, then Sharron and Julie joined in. Before Jesse finished, they were all laughing out loud.

"From now on," the nurse suggested, "you'd better stick to haunting your own floor."

They decided to start at Wendy's room, where a whole roomful of unsuspecting victims waited. Sharron and Julie walked in first. When everyone was looking, in leapt four growling, howling masked men. The only mom in the room let out a shriek before she started laughing. And though Steve wouldn't admit to it, Chipper saw his dad jump at least an inch off his chair.

As the growling waned, another sound emerged. It was Wendy – giggling!

"Grrrrrrrrr!" Chipper slunk to her side, pulled down his mask, and said, "Boo!"

"Hi," Wendy answered.

For a moment the room went quiet. Then, as Wendy looked at her brother and sister and started giggling again, everyone joined her – half laughing, half crying.

"Now we have cause for a three-way celebration today. Chipper and Johnny going home, and Wendy." Steve looked lovingly at the little girl giggling in her bed. "Definitely for Wendy, our number one giggling ghost."

As soon as the Mangums got back to their room, Sharron started digging in her purse.

"Chipper, you need a haircut."

Chipper studied his mom's face to see if she was teasing or not.

"Aha! I knew they were in there somewhere." She produced the small haircutting scissors and started snipping the air. Pointing them at the chair in front of her, she said, "Sit right here, Champ."

Still uncertain, Chipper reached up and rubbed his fuzz-covered head.

"Haircut?" he said, his face screwed up in puzzlement. "Look." His mom was showing him stray strands of single long hairs springing out from the dark patches of frizz on his head. She handed him a small mirror and began clipping. Smiling in spite of herself, she thought how silly she must look, tracing and clipping hairs one at a time. "You're looking good, Fella! You'll have all the girls back home chasing you." His face suddenly lit up.

"Home!" He exclaimed with enthusiasm. "Go home now?"

"No, Chipper. Not now. Tomorrow." Sharron had repeated that countless times already today. His memory was like a bucket with a hole in the bottom. "Tomorrow we go home; today, we go to your party." Chipper jumped up, ready to go. "Hold on! Let me finish first!"

When she finally released him Chipper crouched down and pulled Johnny's present from under his bed, tucked it under his arm, and hurried next door to get his friend. As soon as Johnny wheeled to the door, Chipper dropped the present in his lap. Johnny read the card, then forced his hands to hold and pull until the newspaper wrapping fell to the floor, revealing the prized Nerf hoop. Neither boy said a word. Johnny smiled up at Chip and pushed a button on his wheelchair synthesizer. The electronic voice had been programmed to speak slowly.

"I will love . . . and miss you. Thank you, Chipper . . . for being . . . my friend." Chipper leaned down and gave Johnny a hug.

Warren had done a bang-up job decorating the Rec. Room. The cafeteria sent up a big farewell cake and a couple of gallons of punch. Chipper's favorite Garth Brooks tape was playing in the background, and everyone who could came to say good-bye to Johnny and Chipper. One of the Life Flight crew brought Chipper a T-shirt and a pair of wings. BarDonna gave Chipper a big box full of bubbles and tapioca pudding. But nothing could pull Chipper, Johnny, or Tug from the corner for long. The friends were too busy shooting hoops.

25

Grand Entry

There they were, heading down the road. The road home.

Sharron stared ahead. She'd been in daze all morning. She turned from the car window to look at her husband. His face wore the same winsome smile it had when they made that final walk through the hospital foyer. He felt it too. Mixing with the great joy of this day was a definite undercurrent—the uneasiness of entering unknown realms.

Steve's far-away expression focused and he signaled to take the next exit. With a light twinkling in his eyes he flashed a smile of expectation at his wife.

"Close your eyes, boys."

The boys traded suspicious glances. Scotty gave a shrug and pulled his hat over his eyes. Chipper's whole face puckered as he squeezed both eyes tight.

When the car came to a stop, Steve called, "There she is!"

Scotty's eyes were wide as he hopped out and began circling the sleek blue-and-silver boat. "It's really ours?" he exclaimed over and over. Chipper was enjoying the pure pleasure he saw in his dad and brother. He followed them around, nodding his approval.

Talk of future fishing trips occupied them as they hummed on down the freeway toward home. After awhile the excitement subsided and a sleepy quiet settled over them. But as they drew within a few miles of Cedar City, Chipper perked up. He pressed his nose against the window, his eyes wide and expectant as they passed the big green sign that said "Cedar City: Next Three Exits." Sharron and Steve kept turning in their seats to watch his reactions.

"Here we are."

Chipper's expression was suddenly serious.

"Is Jason home?" He had asked the question several times during the trip. Each time his brother Scott assured him he would be seeing Jason. Each time Chipper had settled back and said, "I love Jason."

"You'll be seeing a lot of friends again, Chipper," his mother was saying, "but not today. We promised the doctors we'd get you right home to bed and keep things quiet for awhile." Her last words came haltingly. She sat forward and looked out the window. "What on earth?"

"Looks to me like he'll be seeing them sooner than we expected," Steve said. He slowed down and steered the car around the exit ramp, stopping at the sign to stare with his family.

Yellow balloons and flags waved above the cheering crowd that filled the Holiday Inn parking lot. Horns began honking and cheers grew louder as Steve slowly pulled in.

"So much for that quiet homecoming," Steve grinned at Sharron. In her astonishment, she had not spoken a word, but sat gaping at the throng of cheering faces, shaking her head in disbelief. Seeing the Asworths' car, the Mangums pulled to a stop.

Sharron had barely opened her door when Chipper bounded out. He had spotted Jason. Conversations stilled, eyes watched. Time itself seemed altered. Smiling, Chipper stood in front of Jason for only a second before reaching up for a big hug. Any sense of uncertainty melted away as Jason embraced his young friend. Arron stepped up from behind and made it a three-way hug.

A teal-colored convertible pulled up. Before they realized what was happening Chipper and his family were seated on the seat tops. The parade began.

Chipper

A police car pulled up and the officer motioned for them to follow. He set his lights flashing and siren wailing. A long string of family and friends followed as the procession honked its way down 200 North and up Main Street. Crowds lined the street, shouts filled the air. *Welcome home* banners waved along with bright pink *You Should See The Tree* hats. Messages flashed on blinking marquees. The telephone poles that lined their street were striped bright with yellow ribbons.

As they pulled into their driveway Chipper climbed out and looked at the stream of cars. Hesitantly he watched the groups of people filing toward him. Scotty stepped to his side.

"They're your friends, Chip. Don't worry, I'll stay with you."

The all-star baseball team reached Chipper first. He smiled and said, "Hi." Scott did the rest of the talking as each boy shook Chipper's hand in enthusiastic welcome. If anyone figured out Chipper had no clue who they were, no one said so.

Sharron was so entranced by all that was happening she didn't notice the man standing by her trying to talk over the noise.

". . . strong person, Sharron," he was saying. She turned and Bishop Higbee took her hand. "After much tribulation come the blessings," he quoted. "Your faith and prayers made this happy scene possible."

"Mine and many more, Bishop. And yours was the first."

Grand Entry

Seeing Chipper in his own room, lying in his own bed, one arm slung around Buddy, and his clothes discarded in a heap on his floor made the events of the past two months blur into a dreamlike fog. Sharron knelt at her son's bedside, tenderly tucking his old blue quilt around him.

"We made it, Chipper. We're home."

Chipper reached to brush a tear from his mum's cheek and replied simply, "Home".

26

High School

"Look! Here comes Chipper Mangum. You know, the kid who got hit in the head by a tree."

"Oh, yeah. Clear back when we were in seventh grade. He looks normal, don't he?"

"Yeah, but he sure acts different. Come on, let's have some fun. Hey, Mangum. Yeah, you. I think you're in the wrong place. This is high school. Maybe you're old enough, but you ain't smart enough to be here. Who do you think you are?"

"Hi. I'm Chipper."

"We know your name. Used to be a hot-shot baseball boy, didn't ya? Now I hear you're nothing but a brain-dead wanna-be cowboy."

"Where's your spurs, Maverick? Or was mommy afraid you'd hurt yourself on 'em."

Chipper's smile faded. He stood in the hall and looked from one sneering face to the next. "Excuse me please, I need to open my locker."

"Got a horsie tied up in it?"

The gang of boys exploded into hoots. Chipper started around them, but the biggest of the bunch stepped in front of him.

"Why don't you do us a little cowboy boogie, then maybe we'll let you get to your locker. If you can find it."

More laughter erupted, but was cut short.

"Oh-oh, here comes Ferguson."

The boys headed for the outside doors.

"Sorry, cowboy Chipper, we can't play with you any-more," one called over his shoulder.

Principal Ferguson walked down the hall to where Chipper stood. He was followed by several other people, including Chipper's mother.

"Were those boys bothering you, Chipper?" Mr. Ferguson asked.

"No," Chipper shrugged.

Chipper

Sharron stepped up. "Mr. Ferguson, if you and the others want to go on down, I'll be right there. Don't start the meeting without me." She forced a smile. When the others had disappeared into the counseling room Sharron faced her son, suddenly intent. "Chipper, was one of those boys the one who pushed you yesterday? Don't be afraid to tell me."

"Well, it doesn't matter," Chipper grinned and turned to his locker.

"It does matter." Sharron was working to suppress the anger welling up inside her. "I'm not going to sit back and allow bullies to harass you and get away with it. If one of them should hit you, or even push you and make you bump your head—"

"Mum." Chipper's tone made Sharron stop short. He looked straight into her eyes. "My head is OK. Theirs aren't. They don't know. They can't help it."

Sharron stood staring at her son. She opened her mouth to respond, but there were no words to say. Chipper smiled down at her, a head taller than his mother now. He put an arm around her shoulder and said, "You'd better go. You don't want you to keep the principal waiting. I'll see you back home."

Lila Bowden leaned forward. "I'm not saying we should set lower standards for him," she said, intensity ringing in her voice. "I am saying we need to be realistic, recognize his limits. For us to pretend he can someday be a veterinarian is dishonest and unfair. After looking at his SAT test scores—"

"Test scores!" Sharron burst in. "Do those test scores reflect the fact that this boy was not expected to pick up a pencil again, let alone take a test? That he was never expected to utter a single word, let alone a sentence? There was a time this boy was expected to be a vegetable for the rest of his life because part of his brain was somewhere on Cedar Mountain! Do your tests show what Chipper Mangum has struggled to become, in spite of impossible odds?" Sharron realized she had risen to her feet and that everyone around the conference table was staring at her. She looked from one face to the next in silence for several seconds before sitting back down. "I'm sorry," she said. "But when people start deciding Chipper's limits, I get a little angry."

"I'm not deciding limits," Lila pounded her fist on the table. "I'm making an effort to deal with them realistically. But if you keep insisting he—"

"Ladies," Mr. Ferguson shot forward in his chair. "This anger will get us nowhere. Everyone in this room wants to see Chipper reach his highest potential. We just need to determine the best way for him to get there."

"That's what I'm trying to point out, Mr. Ferguson." Ms. Bowden had relaxed some, but still spoke each word with emphasis. "I've had experience with cases like Chipper's. I know how to set up effective education strategies."

"We appreciate that, Lila," Tony Loveless, the district psychologist, spoke up, "but we need our combined input to be most effective. Mrs. Laub, as his aide, you've seen firsthand what he's capable of in the classroom. What are your thoughts?" Heads turned in Judy Laub's direction.

The sudden attention caught her off guard, and she shifted uneasily in her chair.

"Well," she began hesitantly, fingering a locket that hung from her neck, "to be perfectly honest, I've done some of his work for him. But that's what I was told to do," she added defensively.

"How in the world will having someone following Chipper around all day doing his work for him help him in any way?" Ms. Bowden was shaking her head in dismay.

"Don't you see?" Sharron struggled to keep the deep emotion she felt out of her voice. "Chipper must graduate! It would be the worst thing in the world for him not to graduate with his friends."

Lila shot back, "So you want him to get that diploma whether he has earned it or not? And then be set free in the rough-and-tumble world believing he has the tools to deal with it all? When the truth is it was all just a bunch of pretending, so he could feel good about himself? We all know Chipper couldn't possibly pass the entrance exams to get into veterinarian school. We shouldn't make him think he could, no matter what his dreams are."

Again the air in the room was throbbing with tension. Ms. Bowden's speech spat out at Sharron like a gust of cold air. Sharron's years of practicing control in the most painful moments were lost. Her voice rose to match the pitch and intensity of the woman across the table.

"If my son puts his mind to something, he can do it. I have seen it happen again and again."

"But have you seen people like your son becoming doctors again and again? No—"

High School

"Can I say something?" Dana Alvey had been sitting quietly for the entire hour, and her soft-spoken manner barely attracted the focus of the group, even as she sat forward, her hands entwined on her looseleaf. "I am not an expert on speech or cognitive matters. But in my experience with the Legal Center for People with Disabilities, I've seen a lot of groups get tangled up in test scores and IEP routines, forgetting the real issue: the human being. Not one of us here is capable of determining Chipper's future, nor do we have that right. Chipper's life is his own. It always will be. He's capable of making valuable contributions to society, but he must be the one to decide what those will be. Our job is to support him, advise him, teach him, but most of all, listen to him. When decisions about his future are being made, Chipper must be given the dignity of being present—of being listened to and taken seriously. Very seriously."

Sharron resisted the urge to jump up in standing ovation. The words became a closing theme for the meeting, and formed the agenda for the upcoming sessions scheduled with the IEP team, which consisted of those present plus one important addition—Chipper.

27

Circles

Chipper was sitting at the kitchen table finishing a tuna sandwich when his mother came in the back door.

"Tuna fish again? I still can't believe you like that stuff." She made a face at him, but his sober expression did not change. He looked up at her, took a drink of milk, then sat back without moving his eyes.

Circles

"So, did I flunk the retard test again?"

Sharron stopped short. "Chipper."

"Well, that's what it feels like. They keep giving me re-tard tests and I keep flunking."

Sharron sat across from him and returned his steady gaze. "No one is giving you *retard tests*, and you are not flunking anything. I've been to SEP meetings and talking with your advisors, just like every other mother on the block this week." Chipper relaxed a little as Sharron stood to take his plate and cup to the sink. "Mr. Ferguson says you're doing very well though he thinks you could even be doing more of your own work, that Mrs. Laub doesn't need to be with you as much as she has been."

Chipper's face darkened. "What if I can't do it without her?"

Sharron sat back down. "There's that old word: *can't*. How many times have you turned *can't* into *can*, Chipper Mangum?"

He shrugged, but the grin spread on his face in spite of himself.

"Remember, no one's going to force you to do some-thing you're not ready for."

"Chipper!" Arron came springing through the kitchen door. "You've got to see this." The two boys disappeared into the living room, Buddy at their heels, and plopped down in front of the TV.

A picnic on Cedar Mountain with the Ashworths had been planned the weekend before, when Steve had re-marked that the woodpiles were getting low. When the call to go came, Chipper and Arron were still glued to the TV.

Chipper

"What is this, a Jazz game or a rodeo final?" Sharron kidded. "Turn it off and let's head for the hills."

"Wait. The movie's just ending. We want to see if the baby's dad pulls the life support plug."

Sharron sat on the arm of the chair.

"He did it. True story, too," Chipper shook his head.

"I don't blame him," Arron said. "That baby only had a twenty percent chance of living. He barely weighed two pounds. If he did live, they said he'd need a bunch of operations and still end up being a vegetable. Would you want to live like that?"

Chipper stood and turned off the television. The room fell silent.

"No." Turning, he looked over at Arron, then to Sharron. "But I only had a ten percent chance and no one pulled my plug."

Sharron whispered, "Dad and I just did what we hoped was best, Son – then said our prayers."

"Thanks, Mum."

The three sat in silence until a blast from the Ashworth's truck horn drew them to their feet.

The crisp mountain air put zip in everyone's mood. It was the perfect season for such outings: cool enough to tinge the leaves with orange, but warm enough to be comfortable even in the back of a pick-up. Shoulder to shoulder, the kids braced themselves for the jiggly ride up the rugged hillside. They were leaping out before the truck had fully stopped.

Arron and Chipper ran for the stump – all that was left of the old ponderosa.

Circles

Steve stepped back a foot or two, squinting in the afternoon sun as he attempted to focus the camera.

"There. Perfect. What a shot, Chipper. The caption should read, *The tree is gone, but the boy lives on!*"

The comment drew cheers and applause from the rest of the group.

Arron plopped down on the stump. "Let's count the circles. Bet it's over a hundred years old."

"Already did," Chip grinned. "Three-hundred-fifty-seven."

"Wow! What a hero. Tackled by a three-hundred-something-year-old tree, and you came out the conqueror," Arron teased, jumping to his feet. "But I'm the king now!" he called, standing like Hercules on the stump. Arron reached down and offered his hand to Chipper, who clasped it and sent the body attached flying off the pedestal to land in clump of tall mountain grass.

"No way," Chipper crowed. "This stump is mine!"

"Come on, you two, if you want to help get wood," Steve called.

"You going with 'em?" Arron asked.

Chipper hoisted the saw and looked out over the mountain.

"Going?" he grinned. "Hey, I'm doing the cutting!"

Love, Chipper

I wrote a poem three months after I was released from the hospital. The poem is called _One Moment_. The last two lines have become a new way of life for me- "Be prepared to accept what is spared."

My poem won the Reflections Contest in literature. A year before, I would have made fun of a boy who wrote poetry. Then a boy would be teased because he expressed personal feelings and truth.

I don't know what my purpose in life is but I think about it a lot and what a great miracle living is. I reflect on life when I watch the sunsets (now that's a real miracle), and when the fall frost is crispy and sparkling on the shrubs (now that's a real miracle), and when I ride my horse in the quiet mountains hearing the sounds of life (now that's a real miracle), and I reflect on life when I feel great to be alive (and that's a miracle too). I don't think I was that way before the accident. Before the accident I didn't care about tomorrow or the beauty around me. I jumped into things without thinking–and I had all my brains then! Now I have parts of them missing and damaged and I take life seriously. I feel I am who I am and if I am happy with it then that's what matters most.

I express my feelings freely without restraint. It is difficult for me to tell a lie. It was explained to me that the lying cells in my brain are missing. If that makes me different then I am happy to be different.

I do not reflect about the other Chipper who had my body. Living is for today, not for yesterday. Yesterday is full of memories—memories I can't change or even remember correctly. Today it is great to be alive and tomorrow is a gift from God.

I don't remember being taught to swallow, sit up, walk, or talk all over again. All I know is now I can do all these things and more. Because I am accident prone, I have had my share of youthful misfortunes, like breaking my nose sighting in a gun with my dad, and cracking a vertebra in my back, and breaking an ankle while four wheeling with friends, and receiving a concussion when my horse rolled over me in a rodeo. As you can see, my life is still full of adventures, and boy, am I having fun! I'm living my life.

Of course, I take all my seizure medicines, I wear the proper headgear (I wear a jockey helmet when riding my horse), I get plenty of rest, and I do listen to the counsel of others. Dr. Walker tried to discourage me from riding a horse—especially in the rodeo. I explained to him that I would rather live to be a year older and be happy doing the things that give me pleasure than live to be a hundred unhappy, bored, and miserable. Dr. Marion Walker (Jack to his friends) listened to my reasoning, set up a bunch of rules, and wished me luck in the rodeos. He really listened to my words and understood the compelling desire of a young boy struggling to be someone. As a father, a doctor and a human being, he is my miracle man who wanted me to have not just a life but a quality way of life. Dr. Walker is a hero and a healer sent to me from heaven.

Since my accident I think I have been influenced by many loved ones.

My Family
When I was twelve years old, my family had the opportunity of shaping a new personality in this body called Chipper.

My parents have sacrificed so much for me. My mom mostly raised me because my dad is usually away earning money to take care of me. Mum is my very best trusted friend who has taught me to love everyone and all things. Because of her journal keeping and a desire to help other families who have head trauma, you hold a part of her heart and soul in your hands. I love her so much for that. My dad is my very best friend who shares everything that is good and just in this life. He is so dedicated to our family that he spells sacrifice: b-l-e-s-s-i-n-g.

I have two sisters and a brother whom I love very much. Karie (husband Nick, children Sean and Nikki) has taught me patience and understanding. She helps me to see the beauty around me. My sister Terie (husband Brad, daughter Ashlie, and soon to be new son) is teaching me to be independent and to have faith in myself. When I am confused and frustrated (which happens a lot to head trauma survivors), she gives of her time to help me through the tough days. My brother Scott (wife Kelly and soon to be little Mangum) has taught me laughter, joy, and happiness. He has taught me to be responsible and to make every day count for something good.

My grandparents, Bill and Mary Barker, who lost their oldest son Norman to head trauma when a crane auger fell on him, have been a godsend to our family, especially to my mom. They bring a lot of comfort and support to my whole family when we need it. My grandpa is a hero to me because he is the best fishing partner I could ever have.

My second family, the Ashworths, have taught me about miracles. They have instilled in me appreciation, forgiveness, compassion, spirituality, inner peace and comfort. My second mother, Evelyn Ashworth, is my mom's best friend and a blessing in my life. She gives her time, talents, and caring heart to me, especially when my mom needs a break. I love her very much.

Friends at Primary Children's Medical Center

The second group of people who have shaped and molded the way I am are all the doctors and nurses at Primary Children's Medical Center in Salt Lake City Utah. They seem a part of me—my family:

Dr. Walker and his team of surgeons did the impossible job of saving my life by putting my head back together.

Nurse BarDonna Collinger, who guided me to a new and sensitive life with her heart of pure gold.

Therapist Mark Cantor, my creator, who instilled in me the gift of speaking, the gift of expression, and the importance of self-esteem. Our hours and hours of role playing have given me the confidence to face the outside world with assurance and determination. I can succeed in life by taking one word at a time and it all started in a quiet, warm room with Mark Cantor and a song. Thank you my friend!

I have a guardian angel watching over me, her name is Dr. Vera Tait (Fan to her friends). She has a special healing gift that warms the heart, strengthens the body, and inspires the soul. Her dedication to the lives of her patients cannot be measured in minutes or hours; it is measured in lifetimes. She cares about every aspect of my life (however, we just about lost her when she saw me competing in a high school rodeo last year!). Like a true mother, her heart stopped beating when I galloped out of the shoots swinging a rope alongside a frisky steer. She is my true and faithful friend.

To the entire family of staff and numerous volunteers at Primary Children's, I honor and salute you. Your example of caring and support helped me to be a good person. You taught me never to give up and to always do my best. I love you all more than you will ever know.

Teachers

I have some very special friends in the school system. Because of a learning disability and a seizure risk, I had two very wonderful aides from seventh grade to graduation.

Loretta Nelson was my aide for three years. She supported me, she went the extra million miles for me, and she was the best educational advocate any TBI (Traumatic Brain Injured) student could ever have. Because she believed in me she kept me focused on graduation. Her understanding of me was profound.

Chipper

In my junior year, Judy Laub came on board as my aide. She continued where Loretta left off, but she had to teach and guide me around my weekend rodeo trips. I attribute my success to a lot of hard work that was continuously drilled into me by Judy. Because of Judy, I graduated with my class, having honors in several subjects. Her leadership and example will be a guiding light to me for years to come.

A teacher who believed in me from the get-go was my pre-algebra teacher, Gary Cowart. He never gave up on me, and he came up with some of the most interesting ways to teach me new theories. For example, I could not understand the concept of figuring angles. Mr. Cowart had me come over to his house and we put up sheet rock in his basement. We had to measure, calculate, cut on angles and put the Sheetrock properly in place. I will never forget the moment when everything clicked in my head; I could visualize what he was trying to teach me and the impossible problem became the birth of a skill. We were so excited we started writing formulas and equations right there on the Sheetrock.

Buddies

The fourth group who influenced me and helped make me what I am now is my friends. Like Jesse and Josie Wood and their sweet little sister Wendy, who was life flighted with head trauma to Primary Children's a week after me. They became my friends while I was at the hospital, even when I didn't look very good and slobbered most of the time. They stayed my friends after I was released from the hospital. It was good to have people I felt comfortable around when I got home. You see, I was different to everyone else. Jesse and Josie knew I could not help being different. We are still the best of friends today.

I have another lifelong friend who will never leave me—Arron Ashworth. Arron never made fun of me, even though I turned into a cowboy, and other kids teased me about it. His love and support have been the cornerstone in my life. Arron and I will be friends united forever. So will Jason, who wrote me a special letter once that changed the course of my life forever. Jason teaches me to make the right choices by the example he is to me. I will always cherish our friendship. My life is crowded with so many friends that I can not list every one of them.

Friends at Work

Eventually everyone needs a good break in their life. My break came in October 1995, when I applied for a job at Quality Ready Mix in Cedar City. David Carter interviewed me for a clean-up/handyman job. He knew of my seizure problems; however, he could see beyond that and looked at the positive in me. I started out working after school to earn money for my rodeo entry fees. Dave Carter went out of his way to make sure I would get company health insurance (which is just about impossible with a brain injured person). He gave me the opportunity to have a trained skill. Now I can provide for myself for the rest of my life. Dave arranged and had first aid training for all employees, with a special section on seizures so my fellow employees would not be real nervous around me. What a great man!

Chipper

My immediate boss was Carl Nelson. He's the kind of boss who brings fear and trembling into the lives of all workers. He is tough as nails and has chased away as many greenhorn employees as he has kept. One thing I did notice was how all the employees who weathered the Carl storms were the best employees. They all have high-paying positions and have earned the respect of everyone, including the respect of Carl Nelson. Through the leadership of Carl, I have learned to appreciate my job. He taught me to give an honest day's work for an honest day's pay. After graduation from high school, I was promoted to a heavy equipment loader operator position. A man-size job with man-size pay. I can't get mushy about Carl because who really loves nails? I do honor the purpose of those tough nails that helped build this boy into a man.

Book Friends

A very special heartfelt thanks to Gayla Schmutz and Lorraine Thompson, the authors of this book. Their compassionate natures and caring spirits have produced the much-needed message in this book. All the hard work, all the night sessions and sacrifice to family and friends are so very much appreciated. I can not express the great love I have for them. The words are sometimes hard to find but I do hug them every time we are together. I pray we are together forever.

A man I have never met by the name of Tom Baker has done all the illustrations for this book. From the drawings I can tell you he has captured the real me. Since I have not met Tom I have imagined in my mind a hero of mine—John Wayne. Tom is my John Wayne. Thank you so much for coming into my life.

Animal Friends

I can't forget two other great friends of mine. Twist, my horse, who tried to shelter and protect me when we rolled over each other in a rodeo. From the beginning he knew I needed him to be the teacher and I would be the willing and sometimes clumsy learner.

And of course Buddy, my dog, who has always loved and treated me the same. Sometimes when I felt very lost and lonely, it seemed like Buddy was the only one who always saw the real me. Man's best friend is his dog. I will live my entire life trying to live up to being Buddy's best friend and companion.

My Message:

I think there is a great need for the message in this book. That is: whatever your problem is, you can get through it. You should never give up no matter how hard the situation gets or how impossible it may seem. You should be yourself too, and let others be themselves. I hope when people read this book they will know more about those who have had head trauma and appreciate them even if they are very different. They are still themselves deep down. I hope people try "to accept what is spared" —it's someone's life!

Love,
Chipper

One Moment

The tree
Enormous and looming
Invited the buzzing chain saw
In the boy's hand
The tree
Cracks and twists
Falling unexpected
Running, running
The boy
Is hit
Struck in the head
Sound of ambulance
Surgery
Pain
Almost dead
Hospital and therapy
The summer made long
Life
Is precious
So watch for danger
Be prepared
To accept what is spared

Chipper Mangum

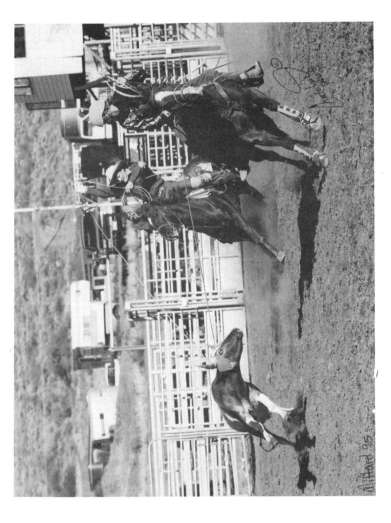

Chipper and Twist team roping in the Dixie Six High School Rodeo, St. George, Utah, 1995.
Photo courtesy of Chatelain Photography, Clinton, Utah.

About the Authors

Gayla Schmutz was born and raised in Cedar City, Utah, where she still resides with her husband, Brad, and their children, Cade, Terrin, Kina, Lehn, Trent, Taylor, and Crae. She has degrees in English and elementary education from Brigham Young University and Southern Utah University. Along with being in the mountains with her family, she considers writing her special therapy, and enjoys writing poetry, short stories, and music. She has especially loved her opportunities to write the true stories of her friends Joshua Dennis in *The Hidden Treasure*, and now, Chipper Mangum in *Chipper*.

Lorraine Thompson claims the red rock canyons and aspen trees of Southern Utah as her native home. She grew up in Parowan, married Mike Thompson, and made the twenty-mile move to Cedar City, where they are raising their five children. Her degrees in social work and child development have been foundational for what she considers her primary focus—her family. Lorraine also writes and performs music about the people and places she loves.

Tom Baker grew up in Winnemucca, Nevada. He and his wife, Gina, and their two children now live in Elko, Nevada, where he is employed with Newmont Gold. He enjoys art as a hobby, with a special love for western and rodeo art. Mr. Baker enjoys illustrating cowboy poetry for many of his friends.

Lorraine, Chipper, Gayla, Sharron and Buddy

"Chipper" Education Packets

It is the desire of Chipper and Sharron Mangum to promote discussion about Traumatic Brain Injuries (T.B.I.), their effects and prevention. In response to this desire, we have prepared an educational packet which includes age-appropriate discussion guides, activities, and Internet sources appropriate for use in public schools or families. This packet focuses on issues discussed in the book including:

The brain, its function and care
The power of friendship
The value of individuality
Dealing with our fears

Please contact us at:
"Chipper" Education Packet
P.O. Box 1588
Cedar City, Utah 84721
Or e-mail:
lthompson@tcd.net